CORE BUSHCRAFT

Disclaimer

The reader is urged to use the information contained in this book responsibly.

The author and publishers do not accept responsibility for any injuries, damages, losses, prosecutions, or proceedings brought or instituted against any person or body as a result of any use or misuse as a result of following this information.

The author and publishers also assume no responsibility for any omissions or errors and make no warranty that the information is appropriate for every situation, individual, or purpose.

Prior to utilizing any of the skills or information in this book, make sure that you are aware of your own abilities and limitations and have researched all applicable risks and local laws.

While practicing wilderness survival, you should also ensure that you are respectful of private property rights of landowners and of laws that protect natural resources and plant and animal species.

CORE BUSHCRAFT

A WILDERNESS LIVING SKILLS SOURCEBOOK

PAUL KIRTLEY

SCHIFFER CRAFT

4880 Lower Valley Road • Atglen, PA 19310

Other Schiffer Craft Books by the Author:

Wilderness Axe Skills and Campcraft,
ISBN 978-0-7643-6148-7

Other Schiffer Books on Related Subjects:

Guide to Knife & Ax Throwing, Dieter Führer,
ISBN 978-0-7643-4779-5

The Global Outdoor Survival Guide: Basic to Advanced Skills for Every Environment, Joe Vogel,
ISBN 978-0-7643-5426-7

Natural Leather Tanning, Markus Klek,
ISBN 978-0-7643-6611-6

Library of Congress Control Number: 2023941466

Produced by BlueRed Press Ltd. 2026
Interior design by Insight Design Concepts Ltd.
Type set in Adobe Caslon

ISBN: 978-0-7643-6759-5
Printed in China
10 9 8 7 6 5 4 3 2 1

MIX
Paper | Supporting responsible forestry
FSC® C104723

Published by Schiffer Craft
An imprint of Schiffer Publishing, Ltd.
4880 Lower Valley Road
Atglen, PA 19310
Phone: (610) 593-1777; Fax: (610) 593-2002
Email: Info@schifferbooks.com
Web: www.schifferbooks.com

For our complete selection of fine books on this and related subjects, please visit our website at www.schifferbooks.com. You may also write for a free catalog.

Schiffer Publishing's titles are available at special discounts for bulk purchases for sales promotions or premiums. Special editions, including personalized covers, corporate imprints, and excerpts, can be created in large quantities for special needs. For more information, contact the publisher.

We are always looking for people to write books on new and related subjects. If you have an idea for a book, please contact us at proposals@schifferbooks.com.

This book is dedicated to Amanda Quaine and Steve Bryant, both of whom have demonstrated more patience than I can fathom.

Contents

Introduction

Psychologist Abraham Maslow's much-vaunted hierarchy of needs is depicted as a triangle or pyramid. Physiological needs form the base of the structure. These are largely basic biological requirements for human survival, which Maslow's theory asserts must be satisfied before we can spend much, if any, time and energy on other aspects of our existence. Competing theories have some of these needs overlapping, rather than sitting in a strict hierarchy. Regardless of the modeling of our behavior based on such ideas, the basic physiological needs of humans, required to maintain biological function, are undeniable—air, water, food, sleep, urination, excretion, hygiene, warmth, clothing, shelter, and light. These are what we need to keep on living. The skills and knowledge to achieve these things necessarily form the foundational know-how for any given environment.

In 1871, naturalist and evolutionary biologist Charles Darwin wrote that a human *"has great power of adapting his habits to new conditions of life. He invents weapons, tools, and various stratagems to procure food and to defend himself. When he migrates into a colder climate he uses clothes, builds sheds, and makes fires; and by the aid of fire cooks food otherwise indigestible . . . The lower animals, on the other hand, must have their bodily structure modified in order to survive under greatly changed conditions."* This is not just a recognition of our basic physiological needs but also a recognition that humans are able to manipulate natural materials to live in the associated environment.

Our basic bodily needs are unchanged whether we are in the bush recreationally or stranded there, wanting to get home. By extension, the skill sets needed to meet our basic needs are the same. Being able to light a fire with a spark requires the same technique when on a hiking trip as when lost in the bush. The hard skill is the same; only the context is different. What is vastly different, however, is the *psychological* backdrop of each situation. It can be argued that an individual's psychology is the single most important factor in wilderness survival situations. If this is the case, then psychology is largely what separates survival from bushcraft.

Bushcraft is a small term for a very large body of knowledge and technique, centered on a practical understanding of natural resources and how to efficiently put them to use in situ. Given the magnitude of the subject matter, those wanting to become versed in a well-rounded set of bushcraft skills often wonder where to start. The most useful bushcraft techniques to learn first are those that are well proven, that can be applied widely using commonly occurring and easily recognized resources, and utilizing commonly carried equipment. Furthermore, these techniques should not take a long time to get to grips with; otherwise they will be useless to most people.

Thus, this book concentrates on widely applicable techniques and knowledge that can be, with not too much effort, picked up and utilized by outdoors people in many different geographical areas. Further, in doing so you will significantly increase your capabilities and competence. This is not a book on primitive living skills, nor is it a survival manual (although most if not all the techniques in this book could be useful to a survivor, depending on the situation). Wilderness living skills instructor Mors Kochanski made the assertion that once one had a sufficiently high level of wilderness living skills, one no longer needed survival skills. To me there are two assertions wrapped up in Kochanski's statement. First, the *hard* skills of survival are a subset of bushcraft skills. Second, the more skillful and the more experienced you are in living in, and traveling through, the wilderness, the less likely you are to put yourself into a survival situation.

This book is concise. It must be. It would be possible to write a whole series of books, each volume about the subject matter of a different chapter of this book. Hence, by necessity of limited space and ease of consumption, the material included here is selective. However, the material is not superficial, nor is it chosen arbitrarily. What is included here I consider an essential foundation for general bushcraft, a set of techniques and know-how that are widely applicable, across a wide set of habitats.

Most of the information is aimed at an individual being able to apply it, either on their own or among a small group of companions. There is also an emphasis on short-term stays in any single location or mobile application while journeying. Larger campcraft projects for bigger groups, longer-term stays, or base camp use are covered in my book *Wilderness Axe Skills and Campcraft*.

If you are a beginner in any of the areas covered by this book, you can view each chapter as an introduction to the subjects. If you already have some experience, you can view this book as a refresh or recap on what you know, as well as a checklist to make sure there are no glaring holes in your basic know-how. There is always more to learn, and there is more on each of the subjects in this book I could share with you. I am also continually learning, from my own experience as well as from the experience and wisdom of others. It's especially important to remain a student of nature. Equally, it's important to be confident in your foundational skills, even if you know you don't know everything. So, dear reader, I offer this work in the hope it helps form solid foundations for anyone who picks it up.

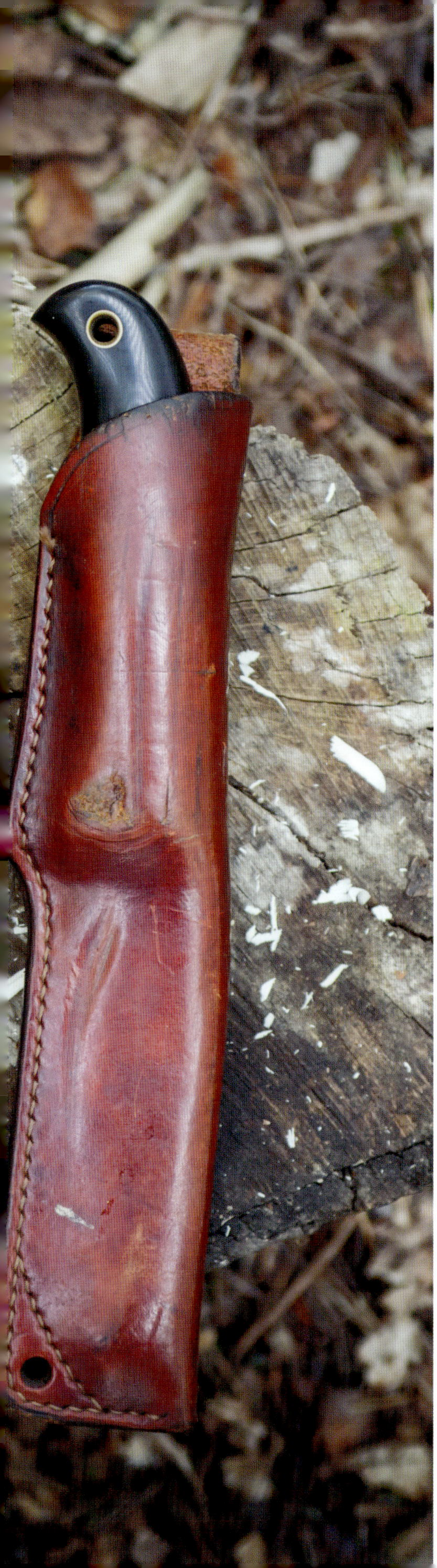

Woodcraft

Woodcraft is central to bushcraft. Much of what we need in camp and on the trail can be made from the trees and shrubs around us, provided we have the right tools and know-how to use them. We choose our tools based on the jobs we envisage and the environment we visit. Further, the aim is to use them with good technique, situational awareness, and a focus on safety.

The ability to cut and shape wood safely and effectively underpins many other bushcraft skills. Using tools lets us harvest green wood, process firewood, shave feathersticks, and create pot hangers that hold. We can also make pegs that won't split, process kindling that catches a spark, and carve valuable items such as utensils. A sharp, reliable cutting tool extends what you can do with your hands, while sound techniques mean you can work accurately without wasting effort or risking injury.

In this chapter, we first examine the primary types of cutting tools used in bushcraft and what makes them suitable for various tasks and environments. From there, we move on to the principles of safe use, before covering a core set of knife techniques and applying them to functional yet straightforward camp items. Finally, we examine how to maintain a sharp edge on your tools. Together, these elements form a solid foundation for working with wood in the field and making the best use of what the environment provides.

TYPES OF CUTTING TOOLS FOR BUSHCRAFT

The primary cutting tools of bushcraft are knives, saws, axes, and machetes or parangs. When choosing cutting tools for use in a particular environment, it is essential to consider the environment itself, the resources available there, and the specific tasks you need to undertake.

Knives are the most general tool of bushcraft. Some sort of knife is useful in almost all environments. While specialized knives with optimized blade profiles might be ideal for specific tasks such as woodcarving, butchery, or filleting, a general-purpose knife should be capable of handling all common tasks to a reasonable degree. This often leads us to choose a moderately sized fixed-bladed knife with a fine, flat bevel. The reasons for this are discussed in more detail below.

There is a great diversity of knife designs.

Machetes and parangs are well suited to tropical environments. These tools come in various shapes, and while they are often described as a large knife, they tend to be larger than many sheath knives. Indeed, designs such as the Kukri are considered a type of short sword, as well as a general cutting tool. This type of tool is efficient for larger chopping jobs such as cutting vines, clearing bush, creating structures, and harvesting food but is still useful for many fine tasks as well. This said, they are often paired with a companion knife for smaller tasks or more refined work.

From top to bottom: Parang, Kukri, and Lofty Wiseman Survival Tool.

Companion knife for a parang.

Axes provide momentum and leverage that a knife cannot. They are particularly useful as the primary tool for processing dense and knotty wood, as well as larger-diameter material that cannot be tackled with a knife. For much more information on the selection and use of axes, please see my book *Wilderness Axe Skills and Campcraft*.

Axes are especially valuable in boreal forest in winter.

Saws have specific advantages over other cutting tools. Saws are more efficient in cutting across the grain of wood, both in terms of physical effort as well as amount of wood wasted. Saws are fundamentally safer to use than an axe or a machete. Being able to saw logs squarely has several benefits also, not least being able to stand rounds of firewood on a chopping block. Whether or not you include a larger saw in your kit, a small pruning saw is a worthwhile addition due to its low weight and compact design. Small saws complement a sheath knife very well. Similarly, a larger saw complements an axe.

A folding pruning saw will complement your belt knife.

A larger saw is a great complement to an axe.

KNIFE CHOICE FOR BUSHCRAFT

When designing or choosing a tool, it's always useful to think carefully about what you want it to be able to do. All the following are important specifications for a knife to be useful for many of the techniques in this book, and bushcraft more generally:

1. **Reliability and strength:** The knife should be reliable, strong, and constructed from stable materials to work in multiple environments. The knife should come with a strong sheath that securely holds the knife and has a reliable means of attaching it to your person.
2. **Easy sharpening:** The knife should be easy to sharpen, both in the field using a small stone and at home using bench stones.
3. **Edge retention:** An ideal bushcraft knife should maintain its sharpness for an extended period; this will depend on the qualities of the steel, including what is in the alloy and its relative hardness.
4. **Green wood cutting:** The knife should easily cut through small-diameter green wood, which is commonly used for creating pot hangers, tarp pegs, etc.
5. **Shaving seasoned wood:** This is useful for paring down dry wood for trap mechanisms, bow-drill sets, and the easy creation of feathersticks for fire lighting—and is dependent on sharpness and bevel angle.
6. **Carving versatility:** The knife should be handy enough for practical carving of both green and seasoned wood, such as for making camp utensils or fixing equipment. This includes being able to create concave surfaces as well as convex.
7. **Food preparation:** Even if it is not optimized for the job, the general-purpose bushcraft knife should still have a suitable shape and edge for preparing small game, filleting fish, and skinning and butchering larger animals.
8. **Compatibility with a firesteel:** The knife should be able to create sparks in combination with a Swedish Firesteel or ferro rod sparking tool.

The above requirements translate to a fixed-blade knife with the following aspects:

Blade length: Opt for a blade that is no longer than the width of your hand, since longer blades can be unwieldy for carving tasks.

Blade thickness: Blades with a thickness of around a 1/16 in. (2–3 mm) are ideal for wood carving. This thickness, however, can be somewhat too weak for other, heavier tasks. 3–4 mm is better in this respect. Thicker blades, above 4 mm, while stronger still, tend to be too heavy for carving tasks.

Blade shape and bevel: A Scandinavian grind (a flat bevel) is well suited for wood carving. The blade should have a gradual curvature of the edge up to meet the back, forming a fine point. If the back of the knife slopes down to meet the point (a drop point), this is beneficial in both strength and functionality of the blade. Avoid significant belly in the blade, since it can hinder fine carving work.

Serrations and sawteeth: Avoid knives with these features. Serrations on either the main edge or the back of the knife will impede many tasks, including game preparation and wood carving. If you want a saw, carry a saw. Additionally, avoid having sharpened edges on the back of the knife, since they limit the ways in which you can hold the knife.

Back: The back of the knife should be squared off to facilitate the creation of sparks with a firesteel.

Tang: The part of the blade extending into the handle is vital for a knife's strength and durability. A full tang, the strongest option, runs the entire length and width of the handle. This ensures the knife can endure heavy use. Needle or stick tangs, thinner but still running through the length of the handle's center, offer lighter weight with reasonable strength, as well as differing handle options.

Steel: Knife steels must balance toughness and edge retention, which tend to be opposing qualities. Toughness refers to steel's ability to withstand fractures, such as chipped edges, while edge retention refers to a knife's ability to remain sharp. It's challenging to improve both qualities simultaneously. There's no perfect knife steel, so compromises are necessary. Wear resistance and ease of sharpening are inversely related, although this also depends on the composition of any sharpening stone being used. The most fundamental choice we must make, however, is between a knife made from high-carbon steel and a knife made from stainless steel. Carbon steel has very good edge retention but rusts easily, while stainless steel is corrosion-resistant but may sacrifice hardness. Modern powder metallurgy stainless steels, such as RWL34 and CPM-154, are better alternatives. In my experience, RWL34 is a strong, tough steel with excellent edge retention that's easy to sharpen. This makes it an excellent option for high-quality knives.

Grip: The handle of the knife should be comfortable for extended use, without causing abrasion, sores, blisters, or broken skin. This means it should conform to the shape of the hand. It should be rounded, with gradual curves, rather than abrupt angle changes, or sharp edges. Durable, nonslip materials that don't feel cold in the hand and can be fashioned into comfortable shapes are preferred. Common choices include hardwoods or resin-based composite materials such as Micarta and G10. Antlers and horn can also make durable, ergonomic, and aesthetically pleasing handle materials.

Sheath: A well-made leather sheath with high-quality stitching and a welt is a solid, traditional option. The sheath should hold the knife such that if inverted, the knife will not fall out. A modern option is a rigid plastic sheath with a positive fastening or mating with the knife. A particular advantage of plastic sheaths is that they do not soak up water. By contrast, a leather sheath can take several days to dry after being submerged in water. A carbon steel knife carried in a wet leather sheath will corrode within hours. This consideration may be more important for a canoeing trip than, say, a hike in arid country.

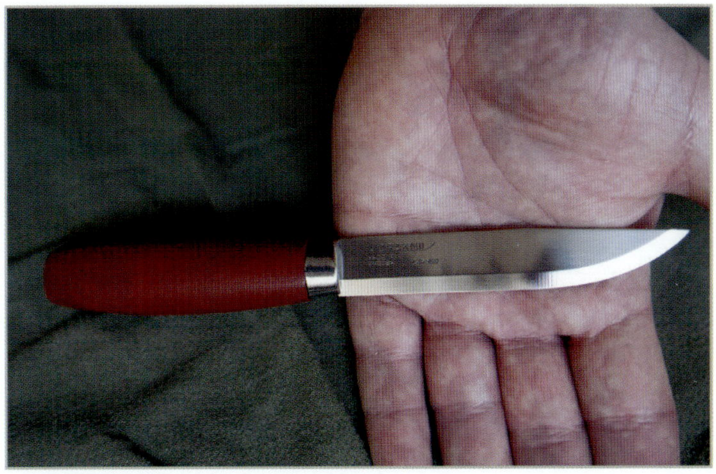

Blade length should be the width of your palm.

Bottom to top: Blade thicknesses of 2, 3, 4, and 4.75 mm. The top three knives have full tangs.

This blade has a single, flat bevel.

The Woodlore bushcraft knife has a gradually curving edge and a drop point.

A custom-made knife with RWL34 stainless-steel blade.

The end of a needle tang.

This knife has a comfortable ergonomic grip and a solid sheath.

Good-quality carbon steel blades are easy to obtain.

Leather sheaths are a traditional option.

Knives with Curved Blades

Spoon knives, as the name suggests, are ideal for carving spoons and other similar utensils. Specifically, they are for scooping out the bowl of a spoon. They have a curved blade with a single bevel on the outside of the curve. They are also known as hook knives.

Spoon knives have a single bevel, on the outside of the curve of the blade.

Mocotaugans, also known as crook knives or crooked knives, are a traditional type of woodworking knife used by North American First Nations. There are many variations. The blade is often set at an angle to the handle in a shallow V shape. There is usually a curved section of blade toward the tip. These knives also have a single bevel, but here it is usually situated on the inside of the curve. Crooked knives that have a straight section of blade and an inside bevel can function as a one-handed draw knife.

From top to bottom: woodcarving knife, spoon knife, and mocotaugan.

The mocotaugan blade is offset to the handle, is curved toward the tip, and has a single bevel on the inside of the curve.

SAFE USE OF KNIVES

We have two safety considerations when using knives: the safety of ourselves and the safety of others. Further, if you are responsible for others undertaking activities with knives, you should have a good grasp of safety principles, know how to explain them, and be prepared to enforce them.

You should also be aware of the limitations of some knife types. Folding knives are convenient but can close on your fingers. Even locking folders have an inherent weakness at the hinge. Fixed blades are stronger and eliminate the risk of the knife folding on your fingers but still have limits in terms of strength.

Pay attention to the following set of guidelines for best-practice knife safety.

Unsheath Your Knife Safely

Keep your fingers away from the cutting edge of a knife when unsheathing it. Familiarize yourself with your knife so you know which side the cutting edge will emerge from.

WRONG: Where not to put your fingers when unsheathing a knife.

Keep your fingers well out of the way of a cutting edge as it emerges from the sheath.

When You are Not Using Your Knife, Put it Back in the Sheath

The safest place for your knife is in its sheath. Don't be tempted to stick it in a log or a tree stump for a few minutes or otherwise leave it lying around. As well as a bad habit that increases your chances of mislaying your primary tool, others may not see it and could be injured.

Since there are plenty of potential trip hazards outdoors, you should replace your knife in its sheath before walking even a short distance. You could cause yourself or others serious injury if you fall with a knife in your hand.

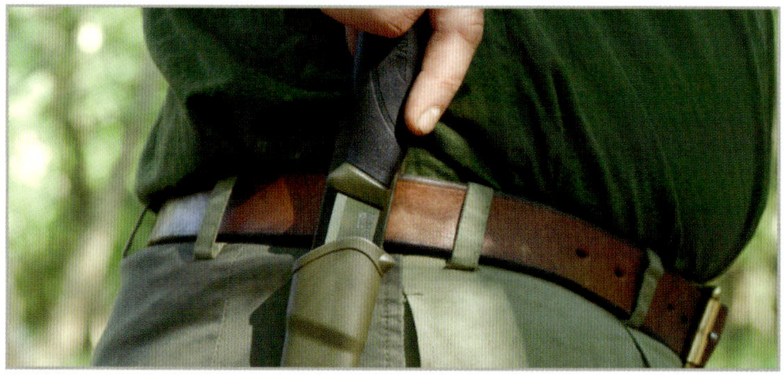

Put your knife safely back in its sheath when not using it.

Give Yourself and Others Room

Don't use your knife in awkward or confined spaces. Give yourself enough room to use it properly. When using your knife around camp, make sure you leave enough room around you to avoid endangering others. If someone is within an arm's reach, they are too close.

Be Aware

If you are using a knife, be aware of the movements of others around you. They may not have noticed you are using a knife. Equally, be aware of others using knives. If someone is holding a knife nearby, make sure you stay at a safe distance. Don't rush around near someone using a knife.

Concentrate on What You are Doing

Many cuts are due to lack of concentration, distractions, or tiredness. If you can't concentrate, put your knife away until you can.

Hold Your Knife Securely

Make sure you have a secure grip on the knife. The basic grip is the forehand grip. This and other secure grips are covered in more detail later in this chapter.

Cut Away From Yourself

Cut away from your body and limbs. Pay particular attention to the position of the hand not holding the knife.

Cutting away from the body and the supporting hand. This is safe.

WRONG: Never cut toward the supporting hand.

Don't be Overambitious

Even with a sharp knife, aim to shave off modest amounts of material with each cut of the knife. Trying to remove excessive amounts of wood with each cut will require excessive force, leading to tired hand muscles and reduced knife control.

Remove modest amounts of material in a controlled manner.

If you need more power, work on the outside of your body and generate power by dropping your shoulder.

Safely create extra power by holding the piece like this, then dropping the shoulder.

If you need more stability, work on a log, tree stump, or chopping block. Just make sure you don't smash your knuckles.

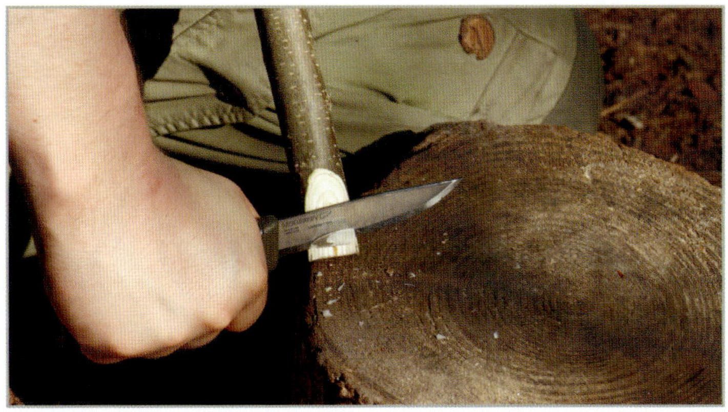

For extra support, work onto a stable log or chopping block.

Elbows on Knees

Your major arteries run along the inside of your limbs. These blood vessels are vulnerable if you use a knife toward these areas. Cutting the major artery in a leg—the femoral artery—is potentially fatal. So, you should take special care not to use a knife in a way that risks this. A particular concern is carving while sitting down. This brings your legs closer to your hands. Keeping your elbows on your knees prevents the knife coming close to your leg.

WRONG: Don't work with the knife close to your inner thigh.

The right way to do it. Working with elbows on knees forces your hands away from your thighs and your knife away from your femoral arteries.

Think About Where the Knife Will Go If You Slip

For every cut you make with your knife, consider where it will end up next—not only if things proceed according to plan but also if you slip off, or cut straight through, what you are working on. Position yourself so that the next thing your knife hits isn't you.

Listen to the Sensible Voice in Your Head

If you feel as though you are using your knife in a risky or foolish way, you probably are. Listen to the voice in your head (or the awkward feeling in your gut) telling you so. Then alter what you are doing so it is safe. If you can't figure out a way of safely achieving what you would like, ask someone with more experience for some direction.

Keep Your Knife Sharp

It may seem counterintuitive, but a sharp knife is a safe knife. A sharp knife is predictable. You don't need excessive force. The knife cuts in a familiar way and you easily achieve what you need to.

SAFE AND EFFICIENT USE OF A SAW

Even though handsaws are objectively safer to use than knives, axes, and machetes, there are some basic safety principles you should follow. These will help prevent minor cuts, particularly to your hands. Saws, especially those with coarse toothing, can roam around on the wood surface before biting into it and establishing a defined cut. You don't want the saw to wander onto a finger or thumb. A simple way to avoid this is to put the hand holding the wood on the other side of the saw blade. This involves reaching through a bow saw or over a pruning saw. Once you do this, the sawteeth cannot jump onto your supporting hand.

Once the cut is established, you can resume a more conventional hand position. For precise cuts, experienced users can guide the blade with their thumb, as with a carpentry saw.

Maximize saw efficiency by using the full blade length. Avoid cutting between two support points, which can pinch and trap the blade. Instead, allow gravity to help the wood fall away, opening the cut. Remember, pruning saws tend to cut on the pull stroke but not on the push stroke. Go more gently on the push to avoid kinking or snapping the blade.

Finally, if there are others around, work together to secure the wood rather than struggling with an unwieldy piece of wood on your own.

Reaching through a bow saw to eliminate the chance of the blade roaming onto the hand. (Jeremy Ray.)

Cut pieces of wood so the excess falls away and the cut is opened, freeing the blade.

Reaching across a pruning saw.

By cutting beyond the points at which the wood is supported, the saw will not be pinched.

Using the thumb as a guide while establishing a saw cut in a specific place.

BUSHCRAFT KNIFE TECHNIQUES

Having a solid set of core bushcraft knife techniques in your repertoire allows you to efficiently perform a variety of common tasks.

The Forehand Grip

The forehand grip is the most intuitive knife grip. It is used for holding the knife while pushing or slicing the knife away from the body, for pushing down onto a block, or in some reinforced knife strokes. Note the thumb is not usually placed on the back of the blade while taking up this grip. Make a fist around the handle, with your thumb wrapped around it.

The basic forehand grip. The essence is to make a fist around the knife handle.

The Backhand Grip

In terms of what your hand does around the knife handle, the backhand grip is the same as the forehand grip. The difference is that the knife is rotated 180 degrees around its longitudinal axis. This means the cutting edge faces the web of your hand rather than your fingers. The backhand grip is used when pulling the edge toward the body and in some reinforced strokes.

The backhand grip. This puts the knife's cutting edge facing the hand web.

Backhand grip in use as the author performs a pull stroke with a carving knife.

The Side Grip

Somewhere between the forehand grip and the backhand grip is the side grip. It can be oriented with the knife's cutting edge facing away from the fingers or toward them. The latter can sometimes be used as a finishing stroke while carving.

Side grip in use as the knife is used in a planing action to improve the finish.

The Chest Lever

The chest lever is a powerful yet highly controlled stroke. The knife is either in backhand grip or side grip depending on what you are working on. The knife always travels horizontally, never up or down toward the body. The workpiece is locked in position by the supporting hand and, sometimes, clamped under the arm too. The knife moves by being pulled through the wood. Don't think about pushing the knife with your hand. Think about pulling with your arm, with the pull coming from your elbow. Indeed, you can move both elbows in opposite directions. You use the muscles between the shoulder blades and a chicken wing action with the arms to create power yet maintain control.

Backhand grip in use as part of a chest lever stroke. The blade cuts away from the body and the nonknife hand.

Chest lever stroke used to remove a side branch.

The Blade Grip

Here the blade is strangled by the knife hand, with the knife being held at least partially on the blade. It should be obvious one does not wrap fingers around the sharp cutting edge. This grip usually brings the thumb down the side of the knife, with some of the blade protruding further.

Blade grip in use, effectively shortening the blade.

Batoning

Batoning is a technique for splitting wood. It uses a knife and a sturdy stick as a baton to strike the knife through the wood. It is useful when you don't have a large cutting tool such as an axe. It is also ideal for splitting finer materials than you might be comfortable splitting with a large cutting tool.

A full-tang knife is stronger and more durable for batoning tasks. Indeed, if your knife does not have a full tang, batoning with it may exceed its design parameters. This can result in the knife breaking, normally in the area where the blade and handle are fixed together. In your backyard this will have little consequence, but in remote wilderness, where the knife cannot be replaced, the consequences may be more significant.

Select wood of an appropriate diameter for your knife, at most ¾ in. (2 cm) less than the blade length. You need to be able to strike the tip of the knife.

A well-made, full-tang knife can be batoned with little concern.

A non-full-tang knife can be broken by batoning.

1. *Begin by placing the knife thus.*

2. *Strike the spine of the knife with the baton to seat it into the wood.*

3. *Continue to strike the blade's spine until flush with the top of the wood.*

4. *Proceed by striking the tip of the knife, keeping the blade horizontal.*

5. *A twist of the knife can sometimes complete the split.*

6. *Continue to split the wood down to the desired sizes.*

If the knife gets stuck, use a precarved wooden wedge to free it. The wedge should have a wide base and narrow tip. Insert it with the narrow end into the split and the wide base outward. Tap the wedge to widen the split, reducing pressure on the knife, easing its removal, and potentially completing the split by prying the wood apart.

MAKING USEFUL ITEMS AND GADGETS

There are some simple items that are always useful for camping out. Plus, learning to make these forms the basis of being able to make other, more complex, items too.

Pegs for Tarps and Tents

Making quick and easy pegs is always useful for setting up a tarp. Wooden pegs can also come in handy for setting up tents on very soft ground.

Create a sturdy three-sided point at one end.

Bevel the other end so the peg doesn't split when knocked into the ground. Quick and easy to make but always useful.

Pot Hanger

While it's possible to push a cooking pot into the side of a fire, it will heat more efficiently when suspended over the flames. Many times, all you need is a simple pot-hanging stick. These work for short stays and simple cooking yet don't take long at all to make. They should be made of green (i.e., live) wood, so that they are both strong and resistant to burning.

A simple pot hanger. Note the end was pointed like a peg before inserting it into the ground.

Detail of how the end of the hanger utilizes a fork to hold the pot.

If you can't find a forked stick, you can still make a hanger by using a crescent notch, using the steps in the following images.

1. *Near the end of the stick, cut across the grain to make a stop cut.*

2. *Slice down to the stop cut. Take care to keep your fingers out of the way even though you have to hold the end of the stick close by.*

3. *Deepen the stop cut.*

4. *Slice out more material.*

5. *Keep alternating cuts until your crescent notch is deep enough to hold the pot handle.*

Candleholder

During the shorter days of the year, evenings in camp are longer and darker. Illumination becomes more important. Candles give off a soft, natural light and are relatively inexpensive. To get the most out of candles, however, it's good to have them raised up off the ground. Making a candleholder from natural materials is relatively simple. This style of candleholder both holds the candle steady and raises it up so it casts light over an area more effectively.

> **Please note:** Strips of bark needed for this project should not be removed from live trees. Removing bark from live trees damages the tree, potentially killing it, and at the very least leaves it open to infection. Take bark strips from fallen logs.

You start with a stick of around 17¾ in. (45 cm) in length. This could be an offcut from making tarp pegs or a pot hanger. Point one end like a peg. Chamfer the other end, so it more easily splits and accepts the bark. Make the chamfer gradual so the candle sits against the top of the surface vertically.

1. Chamfer the top of the holder.

2. NEVER attempt to split a stick like this. If the knife goes too far, you will seriously injure your hand.

3. Split the stick like this, using the tip of your knife, working onto a solid surface.

4. Use the tip of the blade to shave some material from the center of the split.

5. Double over a strip of bark and place it into the split.

6. Your candle will sit in the hoop of bark.

7. *Pull the bark tight so it grips the candle.*

8. *The candle more effectively casts light over an area.*

Carving a Spoon

A spoon is the single most useful eating utensil to have when camping, especially if you have a pocketknife for cutting up food. Crafting spoons hones various carving skills. You'll need a bushcraft knife and, ideally, a small spoon knife.

All you need to make high-quality wooden spoons is a general-purpose knife and a spoon knife.

You can make your spoon just how you want it. Need it to fit into a favorite camping-mug handle? Do you want the handle to have a particular ergonomic shape? Would you like to decorate the spoon with something memorable or significant to you? Would you like the bowl end to be slightly pointed so you can cut into food rather than just scooping it? All of this and more is possible since it is yours to make. Choose easily carved yet durable wood such as birch, maple, or willow. For splitting, select green wood no wider than your knife blade length minus an inch (2.5 cm) and 12–15 in. (30–40 cm) long. Baton the piece into halves to start.

When carving, focus on two dimensions at a time—plan and elevation views—working between them until nearing completion, then blending into a three-dimensional shape for a refined finish.

1. *If you are using your knife to split the piece, then leave sufficient blade proud so you can hit it with your baton.*

2. *Start by splitting the piece down the center of the pith of the wood, either by batoning with your knife or your axe.*

3. *If you are using your knife to split knot-free, straight-grained wood, then some twisting on the knife once embedded will often split the piece.*

4. *Choose the half you like the look of the most. This is a nice straight-grained piece, relatively knot-free. We still want to remove the pith, though.*

5. *Use your knife to remove the pith and to create an even surface from which you can work, a baseline if you like.*

6. *Once you have your even surface, draw onto it the shape of the spoon you would like to make.*

7. Using a saw to create stop cuts ahead of your spoon bowl will speed up the carving process considerably.

8. Next you are going to split the piece down to the stop cut. Rather than aiming to get the split to run exactly for the end of the stop cut, introduce a little bit of margin for error. Observe where you think the grain at the opposite end of the piece connects with the stop cut, then place your knife a little back from this.

9. Tap your knife into the end of the piece with a baton. The split should start to appear and be heading parallel to your envisaged spoon handle.

10. Again you will often be able to continue and complete the split via a twist of the knife.

11. The split successfully runs down the grain and connects with the stop cut.

12. Now repeat the process on the other side of the envisaged handle.

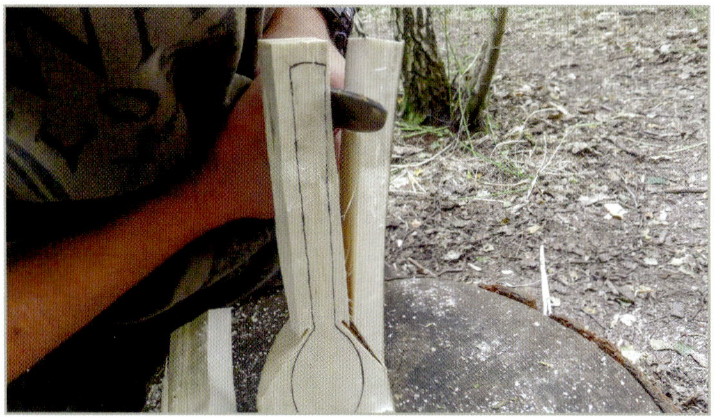

13. Here the split has run off to the side, fortunately away from the sketched spoon handle, rather than toward it. This is why you need a margin of error in case the split runs toward the spoon handle.

14. By splitting away the sides, you save yourself a considerable amount of time and effort to remove excess material.

15. If there is significant excess material on either side of the envisaged bowl, you can also split this away from the spoon. After this last bit of batoning you can start slicing material away.

16. It's worth drawing an elevation view of your desired spoon shape on the side of the piece, then carefully working to this shape.

17. Working on the plan view with the knife, the edges are brought in to conform with the original sketch.

18. The piece is further refined with the knife in elevation view.

19. Once the overall piece has been reduced down to the scale of the desired result, you have a choice. You can either finish the external shape of the spoon and then carve the bowl at the end, or you can carve the internal bowl before making the finishing touches to the outside shape. Here the choice is to carve out the bowl first.

20. Removing material from the bowl before finishing the rest of the handle has the advantage of making the spoon less likely to crack due to drying.

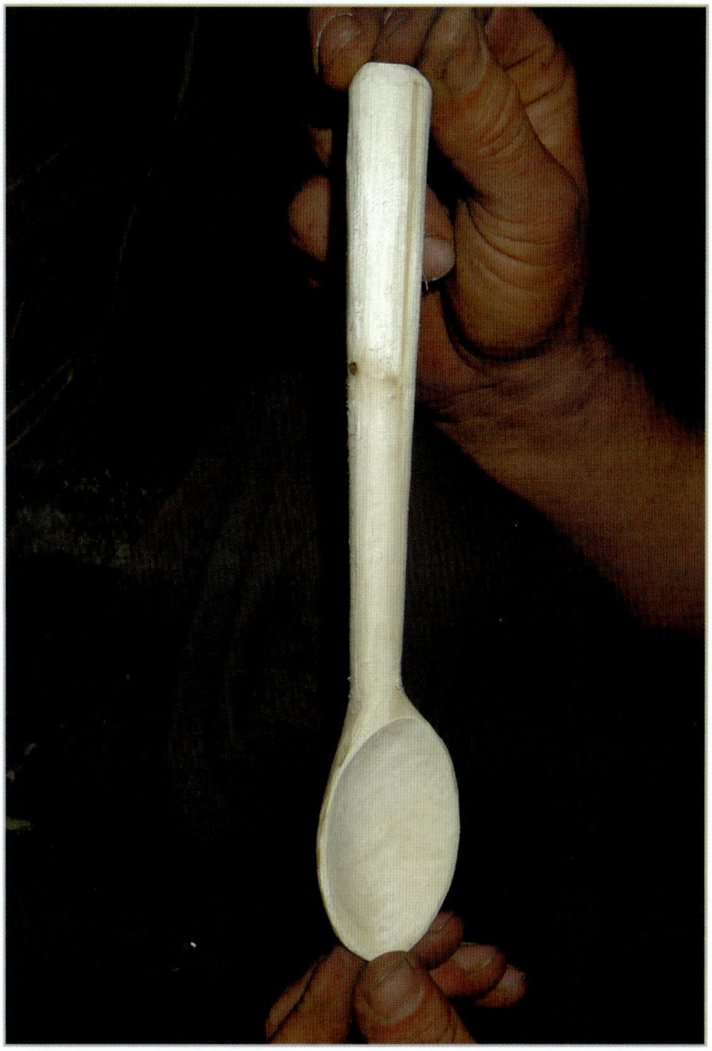

21. After the internals of the spoon are finished, the outer shape was finished with the plan and elevation views being blended together, square edges rounded off, and with a simple, tapered handle.

SHARPENING YOUR KNIFE

A sharp knife is efficient and predictable. When not using full-sized bench stones at home, a small pocket stone suffices on the trail. The principles remain the same whether using waterstones, oilstones, diamond, or ceramic surfaces.

Getting Started

Find a flat, oil-safe surface such as a stump or block. Begin with the coarse side of the stone, generously applying oil.

Apply oil to the coarse side of the sharpening stone.

Achieving the Correct Bevel Angle

Identify the knife bevel and tilt it flush with the stone for the correct angle.

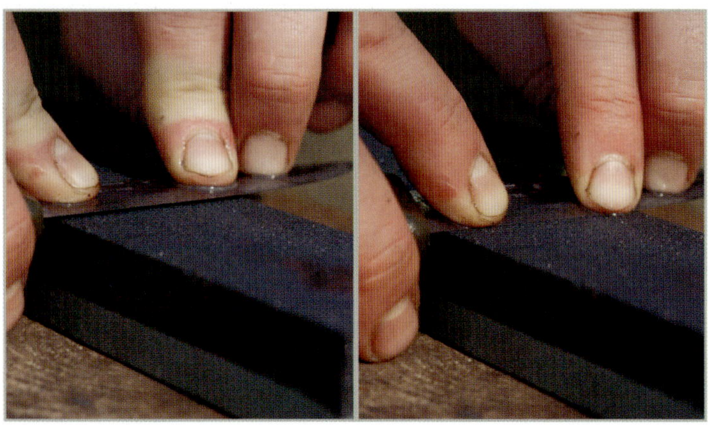

Place and tilt the knife to match the bevel with the stone.

Sharpening Action

Hold the knife at the correct angle and move it away from you along the stone, covering its entire length. For curved tips, lift the handle at the stroke's end.

Above images: Move the knife away and across the stone, lifting the handle for the tip.

Checking and Sharpening the Opposite Bevel

Inspect the bevel for even metal removal, then turn the knife and repeat the process toward you, maintaining even pressure and the correct bevel angle.

Above images: Check for even sharpening, then sharpen the opposite bevel.

Detecting a Burr

Feel for a thin metal burr, indicating both sides have met finely at the edge.

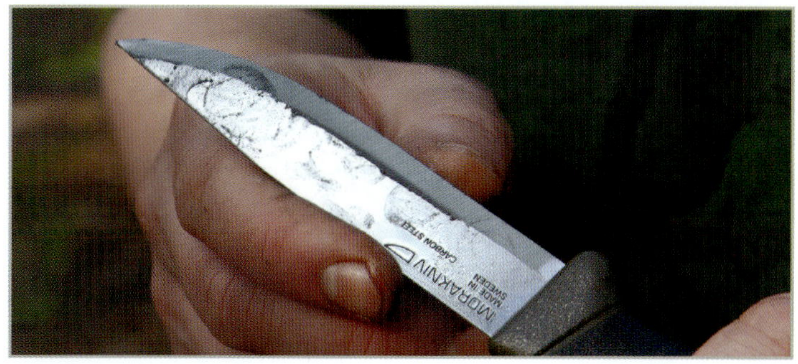

Check for a burr along the bevel.

Sharpening Method

Employ a systematic method to ensure equal sharpening on both sides, finishing with alternating strokes on the fine stone side.

Here's a ten-step process for a bench-sized oilstone:

1. Start with the coarse side of the stone up and apply oil.
2. Make eight strokes away from you.
3. Turn the knife and make eight strokes toward you.
4. Repeat steps 2 & 3 until the edge feels like it has a burr.
5. Make one stroke away from you.
6. Make one stroke toward you.
7. Repeat steps 5 & 6 (i.e., alternating one stroke away then one toward) ten to twenty times.
8. Swap to the finer side of the stone and apply oil.
9. Repeat steps 2 & 3 (i.e., eight strokes one way, then eight the other) three or four times.
10. Repeat steps 5 & 6 ten to twenty times.

Working the knife on the fine side of the stone results in a finer finish.

Checking Sharpness

A sharp knife will catch your thumbprint ridges and reflect very little light.

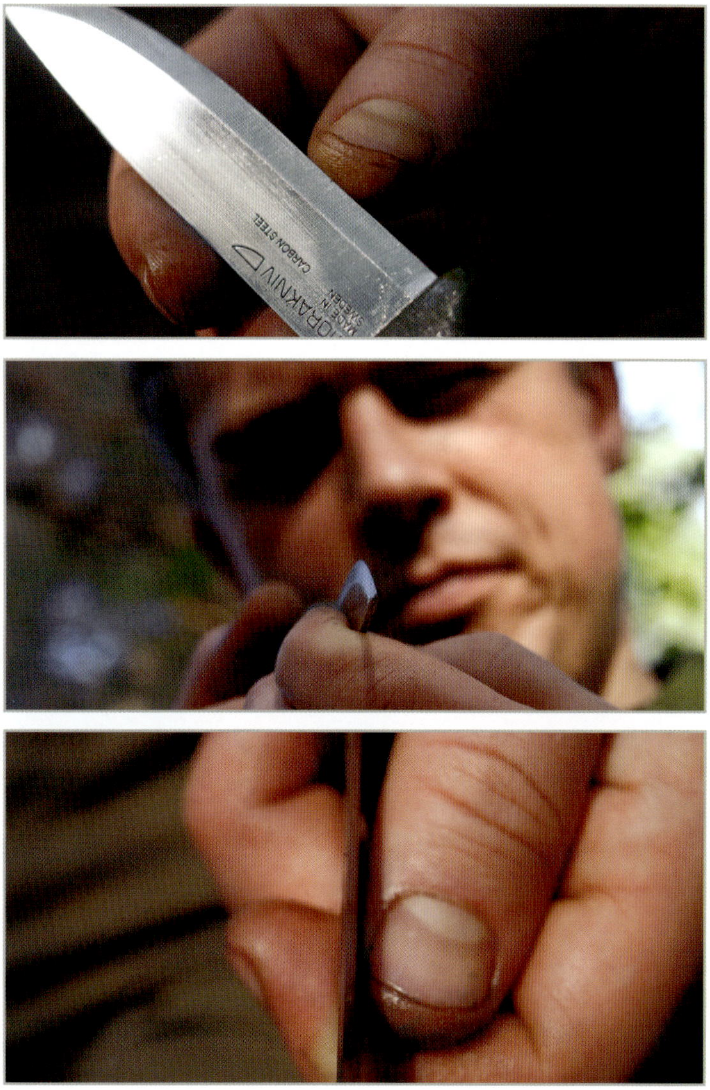

Test sharpness with your thumb and light reflection.

Using Waterstones

Employ the same method with waterstones, using water instead of oil and achieving a finer finish with high-grit stones.

To Finish Off: Belt Stropping

Remove any remaining burr and smooth the edge with a leather belt, leading with the knife back.

Strop the knife on a leather belt, maintaining the correct angle.

Board Strop

An alternative to a belt strop is a board strop. Create a board strop with leather glued to a board. This can also be used with a stropping paste for a more refined polish.

Create and use a board strop with stropping paste for a finer finish.

Sharpening on the Trail

Lightweight pocket stones with diamond or ceramic surfaces, which require no lubrication, are handy for trail sharpening. Simply adapt your technique to their size.

If you sharpen your knife when holding the stone, you have to be very mindful of your fingers.

Use a pocket stone with careful technique for trail sharpening.

Puck-Shaped Stones

For trips using an axe, carry a puck-shaped stone for both axe and knife, employing shorter strokes than with a bench stone, and circular motions for curved blade parts.

Firecraft

The ability to create and control fire at will is one of the things that sets us apart from all other animals. Fire has been central to human survival and development for millennia, and it remains one of the most essential bushcraft skills today.

Fire is one of the most valuable skills in bushcraft. With it, you can make water safe to drink, cook food, warm yourself, dry clothing, deter biting insects, boost morale, and, in emergencies, signal for help. It is also a process we can harness in many different ways, from shaping and hardening wood to melting resins and making adhesives. Fire extends what we can do in the outdoors in a way no single tool ever could. For these reasons, knowing how to light, maintain, and manage fire is essential for living competently in the wild.

This chapter sets out the principles and practices you need to use fire effectively and responsibly. We begin with why fire matters and the considerations around when and where to light one. Next, we explore the building blocks of successful fire lighting, including ignition methods, natural tinder, and fine kindling. You'll then learn how to establish fires reliably with small sticks or by making feathersticks. Plus, when you need to rely entirely on natural means, you'll be able to employ fire by friction. To conclude, I outline the proper procedure for extinguishing a fire, leaving as little trace as possible. This chapter will give you the confidence to start a fire when you need one, use it effectively, and leave a clean campsite behind.

THE VALUE OF FIRE

The ability to ignite and control fire at will sets us apart from all other animals on planet Earth. Fire has played a significant role in the development of the human species. The ability to light a fire remains an essential wilderness skill.

Focal Point for Activities

People love to gather around a fire as a central point for activities, especially in camps. It provides warmth, light, and comfort and can be used for cooking, organizing, and socializing.

Warmth and Drying

Fire provides warmth and protection from the elements, keeping you warm in cold, or wet, environments. This is especially true when combined with shelter. Fires dry saturated clothing, reducing hypothermia.

Producing Drinking Water

When combined with a container, fire can produce safe drinking water. Boiling water kills pathogenic organisms. Fire can also be used to melt snow or ice, providing access to drinking water in otherwise inhospitable environments.

Cooking and Digestibility

Cooking allows us to produce food that is safe to eat by eliminating toxins and pathogens. Cooking also allows us to consume more food in a shorter period, since it requires less chewing and makes it easier to digest.

Manipulating and Transforming Materials

Fire allows us to manipulate and transform various materials, including bending or hardening wood and melting resins.

Morale and Safety

As well as the practical benefits fire brings, it makes us feel safe. When you're isolated in the wilderness, fire boosts morale. Predators are often afraid of fire, making it a useful tool for keeping them away. The smoke from a fire can also ward off biting insects.

Signaling for Help

Signal fires can attract attention and signal for help in emergency situations. Fire can be seen a long way at night, while smoke can be sent high and seen a long way away during daylight.

WHEN AND WHERE TO HAVE A FIRE

Before you light a fire outdoors, it's imperative to consider whether it's legal, safe, and appropriate to have a fire in that location. You should also think further ahead than the moment of ignition.

Legality

Check local and national laws before planning to use fires during your trip or at camp. Even if fires are generally permitted, seasonal restrictions or bans may apply, particularly in high-risk conditions or designated areas such as national or provincial parks. Consult the park authorities for current regulations. Always comply with these rules. If fires are prohibited, prepare for your trip with alternatives for water sterilization, cooking, and warmth. These alternatives include a water filtration system, a stove with fuel, and extra warm clothing to ensure a safe and enjoyable trip.

Fire hazard indicator in Patagonia.

Safety

Prioritize safety when choosing your fire location. Opt for a clear, open spot away from living vegetation, tree bases, and roots. If you don't adhere to this, they can be damaged or even act like a smoldering fuse, taking the fire underground, only to emerge a distance away, igniting the surrounding forest. Avoid lighting fires under overhanging branches or near dry, flammable vegetation. Don't set fires on flammable ground such as dry forest duff or peat; seek nonflammable surfaces such as bare rock, sand, rocky beaches, or dry riverbeds instead. If there's any doubt about controlling the fire, it's safer to forgo it altogether.

Leaf litter smoldering on the edge of an uncontrolled forest fire started by lightning. A campfire could initiate the same smoldering, which will eventually touch something that will flare up into a full-blown forest fire.

During a canoe trip in Manitoba, Canada. There was no fire ban but the landscape was tinder dry. We used small fires, concentrating the heat with a style of fire my colleague had learned in North Africa, which is also very fuel efficient. The fire was on rock and well away from vegetation and right next to a large body of water.

Appropriateness

Appropriateness overlaps with safety but there are also other considerations, which can be highly localized. For example, in parks where fires are allowed for cooking, there are often established fire sites; rather than setting up another fire site, use established fire sites. Even where you are permitted to have a fire, you should prioritize respect for the environment and other outdoors people. This should be central to your outdoor ethics. Even in unprotected areas, avoid leaving traces of a fire if none existed before. This will preserve the natural aesthetic and prevent misguidance of less experienced individuals. Consider whether local resources are abundant enough for fire making without depletion, if there's sufficient water to extinguish the fire, whether you can thoroughly clean up afterward, and if the fire is necessary or just being set out of habit. Weigh the effort of making and managing a fire against the potential benefits. Maybe it's easier not to have one and use the time saved for extra sleep before the next day of your journey?

This sorry mess demonstrates pretty much everything that's inappropriate and inconsiderate about the way ignorant people approach fire outdoors.

Thinking Ahead

Common failures in planning include gathering too much firewood, but also not collecting enough of the right types; for example, too much large wood, and not sufficient small sticks for quick water boiling. Anticipate your needs and collect only enough wood for your stay. Before you start a fire, think about how long you'll be in the area. Think about what you need the fire to do, and how you'll clean up afterward. Toward the end of the chapter, we'll look at how to clean up after a fire. But it should be stated here that the smaller the fire, the less clearing up there is to do afterward. The more you prepare by burning down the remaining wood and coals in the fire, the easier it will be to remove the fire's debris.

Cooking on the coals of a modest fire on a rocky beach by a lake—avoiding damage to vegetation or risk the fire might spread, and it's easy to clear up.

FIRE FOUNDATIONS

To succeed in fire lighting, you must eliminate the reasons why fire lighting fails. More generally, you should have a range of varied techniques and a solid understanding of the foundational principles of all fire making.

> **Two Key Stages**
> When creating a fire, there are two critical stages to focus on:
> 1) ignition to flame and
> 2) taking a small flame and building it into an established fire.

Fire Triangle, in Proportion

To make a fire, you need to understand the **fire triangle**, which is composed of three things: oxygen, heat, and fuel. Each side of the triangle must be equal in size; heat, fuel, and oxygen **must be in proportion**.

Preparation

Preparation is vital to successful fire lighting. Success is largely determined by what you do before striking a match or generating a spark. Put all the building blocks of success in place first. Don't cut corners, even if you are in a hurry for a fire. Proper materials preparation is the ethos of all successful fire makers.

Increasing Surface Area

By reducing fuel size, you increase the ratio of surface area to volume. Whenever you do this to a combustible material, you will make it more likely to catch light from a smaller heat source. It will also burn faster due to more oxygen being in contact with the same volume of fuel. You'll see me applying this principle to birch bark, fibrous barks, tinder fungi, and more.

Going Up Through the Gears

If you have a match-sized flame, you need matchstick thickness fuel. Then you need to add fuel that lights from the thin fuel. Then you need to add fuel that lights from that, and so on. I call this aspect of fire lighting **going up through the gears**. You start in first gear, move to second gear, then third, and so on. If you jump from first gear to fourth gear, you'll probably stall the engine.

Practice

Pre-position yourself for success when you absolutely need it by regularly training in techniques and practices you intend to rely on when conditions are tough. Get into good habits in the good times and they will be part of your skill set when circumstances are challenging.

Good Technique

With all types of lighting, the right technique increases the consistency of success. Increasing the likelihood of your success is the main point of any emphasis on technique. It's not about aesthetics. It's entirely practical. Fire lighting does not reward style. It either works or doesn't. By definition, good technique increases the chance of you starting a fire. Anything else is unnecessary dogma. When I use the word "properly" in the context of fire making, I mean doing things in such a way as to minimize the risk of failure.

Sometimes It's OK to Fail

Failure is OK when you are learning. This is while you are working through a new method, getting used to an unfamiliar body position, acquiring muscle memory of a technique, or experimenting with novel materials. Failure is part of the process. Embrace failure. Learn from it.

Maintain a Positive Mental Attitude

When you employ *any* fire technique, **you must start with the mentality that you are going to succeed.** What is most crucial is that you don't give up. It is imperative to stay positive.

The Best Firewood

The best firewood is dead, dry, and upright.

A Literal Foundation

In most environments, when building a fire you should use a platform of dead, dry sticks. On top of this you will set up whatever fire lay you are using. Creating a platform has several advantages:

1. A platform prevents kindling from sitting on damp or cold ground.
2. A platform (of dead, dry sticks) provides a ready source of fuel at the center of your fire.
3. The gaps in the platform allows air to be drawn into the fire base.

Be Respectful

In the context of bushcraft, fire lighting is not just about starting a fire, but also about doing it in a way that's respectful to the environment.

METHODS OF IGNITION

To create fire, you first need ignition. There are various ways of achieving this, ranging from ancient techniques to modern tools. They all boil down to one of, or a combination of, six fundamental methods: percussion, friction, compression, solar, electrical, and chemical.

Percussion

Percussion is one of the oldest and most widely used fire-lighting methods. It involves striking two materials together to create a spark. In prehistory this would have included iron pyrite and flint. The most common form of percussion fire lighting in recent times was a piece of flint and a specially made piece of steel. This form was commonly used before matches. Even though it is not widely used now, it remains a reliable technique. The spark created is caught and held by a piece of tinder fungus, charred plant material, or charcloth. Charcloth is a carbonized cloth woven from natural fibers such as cotton. This smoldering material can then be used to ignite very fine kindling in the form of a bird's nest tinder bundle.

Spark from flint and steel, caught by charcloth.

The initial spark catch extends to a larger smoldering area.

Friction

Friction fire lighting involves rubbing two materials, normally wood, together to generate enough heat to achieve ignition. There are different forms of friction fire lighting, such as bow drill, hand drill, fire plow, and fire saw. These methods require skill, technique, and practice to master.

Compression

Compression is a lesser-known fire-lighting method. This involves rapidly compressing air and capturing the heat generated before it dissipates. The fire piston, which originated in Southeast Asia, uses this principle. It consists of a hollow tube with a plunger that fits snugly inside. When the plunger is rapidly pushed into the tube, the air inside is compressed. This causes its temperature to rise rapidly and ignites the tinder material placed within the piston chamber.

Solar

Solar ignition involves using the sun's energy to start a fire. By using a convex lens or a parabolic mirror, sunlight can be focused on a small area, concentrating heat enough to ignite tinder. This method can be challenging to implement in areas, or times of year, with weak sunlight but is otherwise highly effective.

Using a parabolic mirror to ignite tinder by concentrating incident sunlight at the focal point.

Electrical

When an electrical current passes through a thin wire, the metal heats up. We can harness this physical process for fire lighting, for example, by touching 9-volt battery terminals to wire wool. The current through the wire will heat it sufficiently to start an oxidization process, which can ignite fine kindling.

Chemical

Chemical fire lighting harnesses exothermic reactions, which are chemical changes that release heat. A classic example is combining potassium permanganate with glycerol. Potassium permanganate is a purple crystalline substance often included in survival kits, since it has multiple uses. Glycerol is harmless and easily available, used as a food additive and antifreeze.

There are of course several other modern, everyday methods of ignition you can use.

Matches

Proper technique with strikable matches ensures efficiency, which is especially important when you're down to your last one. Keep matches dry by storing them in a waterproof container, and shield them from moisture each time you open it.

When striking a match, apply force along its length, not across it, to prevent breaking. Support the head during the strike for better control, but avoid touching it with damp hands.

Pushing down the match shaft plus supporting the head. (Amanda Quaine)

Wind can easily extinguish a match. Turn your back to the wind and strike the match close to the material you want to light. Immediately cup the lit match in your hands until the stick ignites fully, then transfer the flame to the kindling.

After striking the match, be sure to keep hold of the matchbox to avoid loss, damage, or moisture introduction. Place it in your pocket after the fire is lit, ensuring it's safe and ready for next use.

Cup hands and orient with your back to the wind. Keep hold of the matchbox.

Butane Lighter

Disposable butane lighters are common, affordable, and convenient but have some weaknesses. The plastic body can be damaged, leading to fuel leaks. The flint mechanism will not spark if wet. Also it can be impeded by being clogged with debris such as birch bark flakes from pockets or tinder pouches. To mitigate these issues, you can attach the lighter to a cord worn around your neck or use a waterproof sleeve for protection. Butane lighters provide a longer-lasting flame than matches, allowing them to ignite materials that a single match won't. Their performance diminishes in cold environments and high altitudes.

Ferro Rod

A ferro rod, short for ferrocerium rod, is an alloy of iron, cerium, lanthanum, neodymium, iron oxide, and magnesium oxide, designed for creating sparks. Scraping it with a striker shaves off slivers that, when struck with enough speed, ignite due to rapid oxidation. This can reach temperatures of around 6,000°F (3,300°C).

A ferro rod and a striker.

While the alloy will corrode if left damp for a period of time, in terms of immediate performance, ferro rods are effectively waterproof, functioning well after submersion. Further, they are effective at low temperatures and high altitudes. They're durable, with no moving parts to fail or fuel to exhaust, capable of producing thousands of sparks. However, unlike matches or lighters, ferro rods don't create flames. It must ignite a suitable material with its sparks. This will either smolder or catch light. If the ignited material is only smoldering, a tinder bundle must also be prepared. These materials must be carried or sourced from the environment.

Sparks can be generated from a ferro rod not just with the provided striker but with any hard, sharp, and durable edge, including

- metal, such as a hacksaw blade;
- stone, such as flint or chert;
- glass, such as from a broken bottle; and
- ceramic, such as from broken pottery.

A common substitute for a striker is the back of a knife blade, provided it is square and hard. Rounded spines can be modified with a file to work with ferro rods.

Using the back of a knife to strike sparks from a ferro rod. (Duane Yates)

NATURAL TINDERS AND FINE KINDLING

Tinder is any material that can catch and hold a spark. A natural tinder is one that is sourced directly from nature. A tinder does not necessarily burst into flame once it has caught the spark. It may well merely smolder. Indeed, some would argue that if the material does anything other than only smolder, then it is not a tinder. The argument extends to stating that anything that will come to a flame is better classified as fine kindling.

Kindling refers to small, dry, and easily combustible materials such as twigs, thin splints, and wood shavings used to start a fire. A narrow definition of kindling is material that can be ignited with a very small flame but not a spark. But many fine fibrous materials can be used to turn a smoldering ember to flame, even if they cannot be ignited directly with flint and steel. When gathered into a bundle resembling a bird's nest, such fibrous materials are often referred to as a tinder bundle.

I'm not convinced such a clean line can be drawn between tinder and kindling as perhaps there could be in the past. Modern sparking devices such as the ferro rod, producing larger and hotter sparks than traditional flint and steel, have broadened the range of natural materials that can be ignited with sparks. What's more crucial than names is understanding the qualities of natural materials that lend themselves to different functions within fire-lighting processes. Even if you don't know the species of tree, plant, fungi, or lichen, if you can recognize some part of it is of a type that works well in fire lighting, you are well placed to make effective use of it.

Types of natural material that can be ignited with a spark, turn a smoldering ember into flame, or both, include the following:

- Birch bark: thin strips of bark lit directly, or a small sheet or bark with its surface scraped to create fine shavings or dust
- Fine fibrous materials from bark, husks, stems, or leaves of trees or plants
- Fluffy or downy materials from trees and plants, especially fluffy seeds
- Tinder fungi, the fruiting bodies of bracket fungi growing on dying or dead trees, or cankers caused by fungal infection
- Lichen, particularly beard lichens
- Resinous tree sap
- Wood shavings, including shavings of fat wood, which is resin-infused dead wood

Outer Bark Fibers

Fibrous outer barks will mainly be found on trees and shrubs but also vines such as *Clematis* spp., and honeysuckle, *Lonicera* spp. Outer bark fibers can be collected from live specimens to the extent that they are already shedding dry material. Don't strip so much naturally shedding bark that it pulls off living material. Don't cut bark from living trees or plants.

Outer bark of dead juniper, Juniperus communis.

A vine of honeysuckle, Lonicera periclymenum, *shedding dead bark.*

A bundle of honeysuckle bark still needing some processing to break it down to even finer strands.

Inner Bark Fibers

Again, mostly belonging to trees, these are less obvious. These are not to be harvested while the tree is alive. To be harvestable, the inner bark will need to be rotting away from the outer bark and the wood underneath. It will generally be wet and need drying out.

A bundle of dried inner bark from a dead chestnut tree, in the genus Castanea.

Inner bark fibers from a dead branch of poplar, in the genus Populus.

Removing fibers from the inner bark of a dead branch of English oak, Quercus robur.

Plant Fibers

Other plant materials that can be used as tinder include dried grass, dead bracken fronds, stem fibers, fibers from the inside of fleshy leaves, and husk fibers.

Dead, dry fronds of bracken, or eagle fern, Pteridium *spp., are a useful tinder bundle or fine kindling material.*

Dead tussock grass in among other vegetation.

There are many species of tussock grass. The dead leaves tend to sit suspended up in the tussock, so can be quite dry.

Seeds of fireweed, Chamerion angustifolium.

Dead stems of cleavers, Galium aparine.

Cotton grass, in the genus Eriophroum.

Fluffy Seeds

Many seed heads of plants, particularly fluffy ones, will accept a spark from a ferro rod once they are sufficiently dry and teased out. Also, some can be charred and then accept a spark from a flint and steel.

Fluffy seeds of cattails, Typha *spp., will ignite from a spark.*

Seeds of Clematis vitalba.

Tinder Fungi

These are typically bracket fungi. For example, horse's hoof fungus, *Fomes fomentarius*, and cramp balls, *Daldinia concentrica*, are suitable both for catching sparks and keeping an ember glowing for a while. Birch canker, also known as chaga, caused by *Inonotus obliquus*, is another excellent tinder.

Horse's hoof fungus, Fomes fomentarius, *on a birch tree in northern Sweden.*

Horse's hoof fungus cut away to show cross section. The part for fire lighting is the tan-colored trama layer.

A slice of F. fomentarius *trama layer, scraped up to make it fluffier and more accepting of a spark.*

Smoldering slice of F. fomentarius *trama layer.*

Daldinia concentrica, *or cramp balls.*

Birch canker, or chaga.

A lump of chaga.

Shavings of chaga smoldering after accepting a spark.

Lichen

Many lichen species have a fine fibrous structure that renders them ideal for use as natural tinder. Once dry, these lichens can catch a spark easily. Elongated, wispy, so-called beard lichens in genera such as *Usnea* and *Alectoria* are among the best lichens for fire starting.

Lichen growing on a tree in Scotland.

Beard lichen, northern Scandinavia.

Resin and Resinous Wood

Resin is a thick, viscous substance secreted by certain trees, particularly conifers. Resin serves as a natural defense mechanism for trees, protecting them from insects and pathogens. The resin is composed of a complex mixture of volatile organic compounds. Resin is highly flammable and burns hot and long. To use resin as a fire starter, collect it from trees such as spruce, *Picea* spp., pine, *Pinus* spp., or fir, *Abies* spp., by breaking off small pieces of the hardened substance. These pieces can be placed on top of kindling or other dry, combustible materials to ignite a fire. Sometimes you will also find resin-infused dead branches or tree trunks, commonly referred to as fat wood. Shavings of such wood are highly flammable.

A piece of fat wood from a dead pine branch.

Lighting Birch Bark with a Ferro Rod

Fine strips of birch bark might ignite from the sparks of a ferro rod, but a sheet of bark is unlikely to catch. To prepare a sheet of birch bark, scrape the outer surface to produce fine slivers. You can use a knife, ferro rod striker, or any sharp edge that will take material off the bark.

Using a ferro rod striker to scrape the outer surface of the birch bark.

Support the end of the ferro rod on the bark, just behind your pile of bark shavings. Push big sparks directly down at your shavings. Be careful not to strike the pile with your fingers or the striker, which could extinguish any ignition.

You can also push big sparks with the back of a fixed-blade knife.

Birch shavings alight after accepting a spark.

Preparing Fibers for a Bird's Nest Tinder Bundle

The purpose of a bird's nest tinder bundle is to ignite fine kindling from a smoldering ember. This process involves forcing air into the bundle to increase oxygen supply, thus accelerating combustion. Materials such as dry grass or bracken require no preparation. Other fibrous materials need to be broken down into finer fibers by pulling, twisting, rubbing, or buffing them into a fluffy mass. If materials are damp, dry them using available warmth and airflow. Even weak sunshine and a cool breeze can accelerate drying.

Aim for a tinder bundle roughly the size of a cantaloupe melon. For grass or bracken, I would recommend using a bit more to ensure a long, hot burn and protect your fingers while holding the bundle.

Dry, dead grass can be used directly.

Other fibrous materials need some processing after being collected.

Inner bark of sweet chestnut, Castanea sativa, *placed in the crook of a birch tree to be dried by sunlight and breeze.*

A good-sized bundle of fibers.

Pulling apart strips of inner bark into narrower strips.

Working the strips to reduce them to a fluffy ball of fine fibers.

Blowing a Tinder Bundle to Flame

With an ember from any source like charcloth, tinder fungus, or a bow-drill set, follow these steps to ignite a tinder bundle:

1. ***Prepare your tinder bundle:*** *Gather enough dry material and form a nest, with a depression in the center for the ember. Do this before creating your ember. Then keep the bundle dry.*

2. ***Secure the ember:*** *Place the ember into the tinder bundle's center and gently enclose it in the material. Ensure close contact to encourage ignition.*

3. ***Create airflow:*** *Hold the bundle at a 6–8 in. (15–20 cm) distance from your face and blow steadily, as if whistling, to increase oxygen flow.*

4. ***Gentle and consistent breathing:*** *Blow softly and steadily, nurturing the ember without dislodging or damaging it. Waft the bundle in the air when inhaling to maintain airflow and avoid smoke inhalation.*

5. ***Observe and adjust:*** *Monitor the ember's glow and the smoke produced. If the ember weakens, blow more accurately, gently, or both. As bundle material is consumed nearest the ember, press the material inward to feed the ember.*

6. ***Nurture the flame:*** *As the ember catches, continue controlled blows, increasing intensity as the smoke thickens. Keep blowing until the bundle bursts into flames.*

7. ***Establish the flame:*** *Once you have a flaming bundle like this, move it to your fire lay, inverting it to ensure the unburnt base catches. Add your kindling as soon as possible.*

SMALL-STICK FIRE

Once you have a flame, you need to create an established fire. The small-stick fire is the method I use most often and is most likely the method you'll employ at least 95 percent of the time too. It works in most situations in a wide range of environments. As long as you can collect thin, dead, dry sticks as your kindling, you can use this method. The best dead sticks you can gather are either still attached to a tree or hung up in one. This way, you avoid collecting sticks from the ground, which are likely to be damp. For fine kindling, you should opt for matchstick-thickness sticks. They should break cleanly with a crisp and definite click; this proves they are thoroughly dried.

Fine sticks from dead heather.

Search for dead, dry sticks for your kindling. You often find dead branches low down on evergreen conifers.

To ensure success, particularly in wet weather, collect at least an armful of kindling like this.

Matchstick-thickness twigs make great fine kindling.

Break off the small matchstick-thin twigs from the branches you have collected. Create a bundle like this. Keep the twigs long.

*The best twigs from deciduous trees are from birches (*Betula*).*
Collect a bundle of the thinnest dead, dry twigs you can find.

After your initial kindling is ablaze, you need some larger fuel. Pencil thickness is appropriate for the next stage, then finger thickness, then thumb thickness. The idea is for each fuel grade to easily ignite from the previous. You can't light a log with a match. There needs to be intermediate fuel sizes. All of your fuel should be dead and dry. Make sure you collect and sort out your fuel before lighting your fire.

Sort your larger fuel into similar grades of thickness.

Select an area for your fire. In the area where you will have your fire, clear the leaf litter and other dead foliage away until the bare earth is exposed. You should create a platform of dead, dry sticks of thumb thickness. On top of this you will create your fire lay.

Clear the area of dead foliage, down to bare earth.

Lay down a platform of dry, dead wood.

Now that you've prepared the area and platform, divide your kindling bundle into two generous handfuls, keeping it long so each resembles a miniature witch's broom. Mind the wind direction. Kneel with your back to it, placing the kindling in a V shape facing you. Keep your knees and feet together to shield the fledgling fire from breezes.

Keep your kindling sticks long. You can organize and maneuver them easily. Set two handfuls to cross over in the center of your platform like this.

Now, create a flame. Let's use a match for illustration and start by considering how to light the kindling directly. Heat rises, so aim to ignite the kindling low down, ideally at the center of the V-notch where the kindling overlaps, creating a fuel-rich area and a thermal column as it burns. Lighting multiple spots enhances success. If you are lighting a tinder bundle first, place it on the platform, ignite it, then add fine kindling on top.

Lighting the kindling.

Long kindling offers adjustability as your fire grows. You might need to reposition the sticks or lift them slightly to increase airflow and fuel the flames. Practice these adjustments; their impact is significant.

Keeping your kindling long allows you to move it wholesale into the flames if necessary.

Once the flames are strong, add more fuel in bundles, mirroring your initial arrangement. Long sticks can be adjusted without burning your hands.

As the flames take hold of the smaller sticks, add the next thickness of fuel to your fire.

Your fire is now ready to use or build upon. For larger fires, keep adding more and larger fuel. For simple tasks such as boiling water, finger-thick sticks suffice. Remember, thorough preparation and material selection are key, especially in adverse weather. Proper technique upfront saves time and effort.

Small-stick fire established in pouring rain.

Additional Tips

If your fire struggles to ignite, even with dry kindling, a simple trick to boost oxygen is lifting the long kindling sticks. This creates space between the bundles and the platform, enhancing combustion.

Lifting up kindling to introduce more oxygen accelerates combustion.

In very wet conditions, use a double layer of platform sticks, laid at right angles for better insulation. For fires starting with small flames, add birch bark, fat wood, or resin to drive moisture away from the kindling and enhance ignition.

This fire was started in wet conditions by taking a match to birch bark, then birch kindling twigs. Note also the double platform underneath the fire.

During heavy rain, seek natural shelters such as dense foliage. However, drips can still be a problem. Shield the initial stages of your fire with a plastic bag or jacket to prevent water from extinguishing matches or dampening early flames.

Holding jacket over the fire lay to protect the early stages of ignition.

FEATHERSTICKS

Feathersticks, unlike less effective fuzz sticks, are ideal when the small-stick fire method is not available to you. They ignite easily with a small flame or ferro rod sparks. A high-quality featherstick features long, curled shavings clustered at one end, forming a kindling bundle with an attached handle for easy use.

A high-quality featherstick made by the author.

Fuzz sticks are inferior to feathersticks.

Making Feathersticks

Select straight-grained, knot-free wood and cut it into 12–14 in. (30–35 cm) sections. Split these into quarters or eighths, depending on the diameter. Remove any damp outer bark or wood.

Method 1

Prepare the inner edge of your split wood, which remains dry even after heavy rain. Create a smooth, even foundation for shaving curls. This foundational surface is key for consistent, neat curls.

To do this, secure the wood splint upright on a firm surface. Use your knife to level the top by removing any high points. Using the part of your knife blade near the handle, carve downward to create uniform curls. As shavings accumulate at the base, push them away to avoid clutter.

Ensure all curls end at the same point on the stick. Avoid progressively starting lower or finishing higher on the stick with each curl, since this will result in shorter, less effective curls. Consistency is crucial for a cluster of thin, easily ignited curls.

Once comfortable with the basic downward shaving motion, aim to create shavings in a 180-degree arc on one side of the stick. This can be achieved by sequentially shaving down the ridges between the flat surfaces created by previous shaving. Avoid shaving around the entire base, though.

Once you have become consistent with the standard downward motion, you can vary curl placement by using knife angle. Normally, curls align with the stick; to adjust their direction, angle your knife's tip up or down during the cut. Alternate between tip-up, tip-down, and horizontal cuts along the stick's center to fill gaps. Repeat this process, varying the angles, to create an array of curls. In this way you will achieve a dense curl cluster.

1. *You can produce all the sizes of fuel you need to establish your fire.*

2. *In the absence of an axe, use your knife and a baton to create all the split wood you need.*

3. *Split the rounds down into quarters or eighths, depending on their diameter.*

4. *Shave off the damp outer layers as necessary.*

5. *Start to shave off raised or rough sections, which make the wood uneven.*

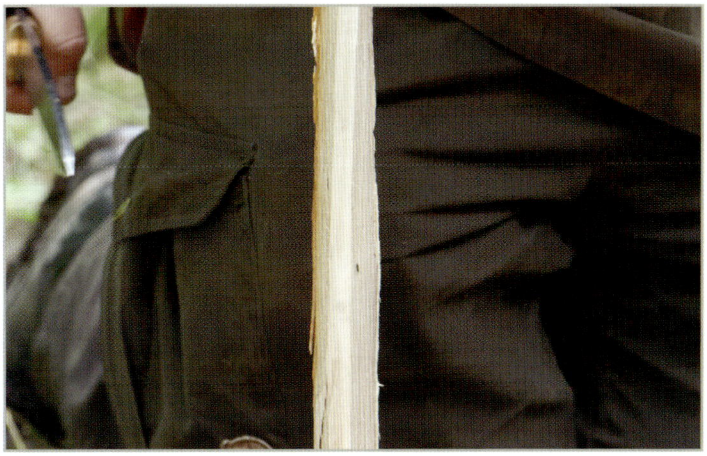

6. *After a few runs down the stick, you will have a much more even surface to work from.*

7. *Now shave steadily downward to create a neat, even curl.*

8. *Placing the stick on a firm surface, work downward with your knife creating shavings.*

9. *You should aim to create a 180-degree arc of curls on one side of the featherstick.*

10. *With the knife tip up, curls move off toward the tip.*

11. *With the knife tip down, the curls move toward the handle.*

12. *In varying the angle and starting and finishing in the same place, you end up with a dense bundle of curls at the end of your featherstick.*

Method 2

Hold the knife stationary and move the wood against the blade. This method, useful without a solid surface, provides more control over bevel angle and curl consistency. Both methods follow the same principles, so practice to find your preference.

1. *Start by clamping your knife hand to the outside of your knee and leave room for the wood underneath the knife.*

2. *Pull the piece of wood back toward you while holding your knife static.*

3. *Angling the tip of the knife will have the same effect as in method 1.*

4. *Again, aim for a mass of curls at the end of the featherstick, through an arc of up to 180 degrees.*

5. *Showing arm positions from a different angle.*

Lighting a Fire with Feathersticks

Feathersticks act as kindling and fuel, relying on thin necks to ensure the curls ignite the stick. Use two feathersticks in dry conditions, four in damp and cold, and up to six in very wet weather.

Prepare the fire lay with clear ground and a split-wood platform. Arrange the feathersticks in a V shape with the open side facing any breeze, and the shavings concentrated in the center of the V. Have small-to-medium-sized fuel ready, with larger pieces on hand.

Introduce a small flame to multiple points at the base of the curls. The flames should spread through the curls and ignite the stick's neck. Gradually add splints and progressively larger fuel, maintaining the V-shape arrangement to build the fire.

2. *Using batoning you can split down to the various sizes of fuel you need.*

When the necks of your feathersticks are not thin enough, the curls burn off but only char the body of the stick.

3. *Kneel in front of the platform, with your back to any wind.*

1. *After clearing the ground, lay down a platform.*

4. *Lay down the feathersticks, alternating left and right of the V.*

5. *V-shaped featherstick fire lay with curls on the inside.*

6. *Ready to introduce a small flame to the feathersticks.*

7. *Introduce the flame to various points at the base of the featherstick curls.*

8. *While you can manipulate the feathersticks if necessary, resist the urge to fiddle around with the fire unnecessarily.*

9. *All parts of the feathersticks are ablaze.*

10. *Once the flames are well established among feathersticks, add your splints.*

11. *Splints added to the burning remains of feathersticks, the sticks of which are well alight.*

12. *The alternating arrangement of the V-structure seen from the side.*

FIRE BY FRICTION

Friction fire involves rubbing woody materials together to generate heat. The goal is to produce a smoldering pile of hot dust that consolidates into an ember, which can then ignite a tinder bundle.

Friction fire techniques fall into three categories, which are based on the direction of friction relative to the wood grain: along the grain (e.g., fire plow), across the grain (e.g., fire saw), or rotationally into the grain (e.g., hand drill). Rotational methods are the most versatile, applicable across regions and wood types.

The bow-drill method is the most widely applicable rotational technique, effective even in damp or cold environments and with various wood species. It is a core technique and the focus of this section.

The bow drill offers mechanical advantages by separating rotational motion from downward pressure, unlike hand drills, which require specific hand conditioning. However, it involves a more complex apparatus and demands high-quality cordage.

Using a bow drill requires coordination and perseverance but becomes a reliable one-person method once mastered. It can also be adapted for two or three people, making it easier in challenging conditions such as high humidity. Developing proficiency with the bow drill provides a solid chance of achieving fire by friction wherever suitable woody flora is available.

Bow-drill components: bow, bearing block, spindle, ember pan, and hearth board.

Bow set assembled and in use.

Bow-drill body position.

Bow Drill: A Guide to Success

Selecting Materials

Selecting the right materials is vital for bow-drill success. Familiarize yourself with common deciduous hardwoods such as willow (*Salix*), alder (*Alnus*), birch (*Betula*), and maple (*Acer*), which are widespread and easy to identify. Evergreen softwoods such as pine (*Pinus*), spruce (*Picea*), larch (*Larix*), and fir (*Abies*) are also valuable. Lime and basswood (*Tilia)*, cedar (*Thuja*), and juniper (*Juniperus*) work well but may be less common in some areas. Avoid hard hardwoods such as oak (*Quercus*), beech (*Fagus*), hornbeam (*Carpinus*), and chestnut (*Castanea*), and fruit woods such as apple (*Malus*), pear (*Pyrus*), and hawthorn (*Crataegus*), which are too dense for friction fire lighting.

For the spindle and hearth, select dead, dry, standing wood. Upright wood is driest, while angled or fallen wood is often damp. Moisture significantly reduces your chance of success, so prioritize the driest materials available.

When learning, use the same wood type for both components to minimize variables. The wood's hardness is key; too hard and it will be difficult to generate the dust required to make up an ember. Too soft and your set will literally disintegrate as you use it. You should be able to just make an impression in any wood of suitable hardness (the wood itself, not the bark) with your thumbnail.

Thumbnail test on potential bow-drill wood.

The bow should be lightweight, strong, rigid, and slightly curved, with a length from your fingertips to your sternum for efficient strokes. The bearing block should be green wood from a hard species or, if available, a rock with a suitable depression.

Length of the bow: fingertips to sternum.

Gather more tinder than you think necessary. Establishing a fire requires not only igniting a tinder bundle but also sustaining enough heat to ignite small sticks.

Cordage is often the limiting factor. It's the hardest component to improvise, especially in winter. While plant fibers can work, they are less durable and require precise technique. Traditional rawhide or modern synthetic options such as paracord offer better durability and grip on the spindle.

Making Your Bow-Drill Set

Precision is key when carving your spindle. It must be straight and round. Aim for 6–8 in. (15–20 cm) length. The diameter should not exceed 1 in. (2.5 cm), about the width of your thumb's knuckle. Except for the pointed top and blunted base, maintain consistent thickness throughout. The spindle must be cylindrical for consistent cord grip and smooth rotation.

1. *Carve your drill dead straight.*

2. *Bring the spindle top gradually to a sharp point. A bevel can be added for resilience.*

3. *Bring the spindle bottom to a shallow point.*

The hearth's thickness should approximate to your spindle's diameter. Too thin, and you risk drilling through; too thick, and the dust may cool before forming an ember.

4. Spindle, "floorboard" hearth, and carved ember pan.

If the hearth will be used repeatedly, create a well-crafted board for multiple uses. For immediate fire making, simply ensure stability and proper thickness at one end before drilling.

5. Note the top of this hearth board is cleaned at only one end.

Putting It All Together

Place your spindle on the outside of the cord. Twist your spindle into the cordage so that the spindle is on the outside of the cord, not between the cord and the bow. This allows the full length of the cord to be used.

Make sure the cord grips the spindle. When you have twisted your spindle into your bow string, grab the spindle in one hand and your bow in the other and try to slide the spindle up and down the cord. If it slips at this point, it will slip when you are drilling. If it is slipping, remove the spindle, retighten the cord, then try again.

Lubricate the bearing block. Add a small amount of green leaf material or spit into the depression in your bearing block for lubrication. Alternatively, if your face is greasy enough, you can rub the pointed top of the spindle on your face to add extra lubrication. The best place is on either side of your nose.

Burn in your set before you cut the notch. If you cut the notch first, the drill can drift away from the notch as it beds into the hearth. This will cause problems. Burn in the set first, then cut the notch.

The set is burnt in when the depression in the hearth and the whole of the bottom of the drill is black (not brown). You shouldn't need to go flat out to burn in the set. Don't get too pumped at this stage.

Once you start drilling, start off steadily, warming up both yourself and the bow-drill set. Make sure your rhythm is steady and you use the full length of the cord, not just the central portion.

The bow should be kept horizontal, moving parallel to the ground. This will keep the cord in the middle of the spindle and help prevent the spindle from popping out. The motion should come from your shoulder, not the elbow.

The bow should run horizontal, parallel to the ground.

The notch should be one-eighth of the circle you have drilled into the hearth. The sides of the notch should be smooth and meet at the center of the circle. Mathematically, you are cutting out a sector of the circle with a central angle of 45 degrees. If the notch is too small, it can be hard to consolidate enough hot dust to form an ember. If the notch is too big, the spindle can easily jump out of the depression.

Once the set is burned in, cut a notch one-eighth of the circle.

Cut the notch on the side of the hearth that is nearest to you. This allows you to see the dust gathering in the notch. Cut the notch facing away from you, and you won't see a thing.

Cut the notch on the side of the hearth board closest to your body, so you can see into it.

Making Fire with a Bow Drill

Preparation: Prepare your fire site with tinder, kindling, and fuel ready to use. Place a wood chip or bark beneath the hearth to catch dust and hold the ember. Comfort and stability are crucial. Secure the hearth with your foot and brace your bearing block arm against your shin for support.

Technique: Begin with a steady rhythm, applying the pressure needed to produce smoke during the burn-in phase. Use long, consistent strokes to generate thick smoke at the spindle's base. Once thick smoke appears, increase your speed for at least ten additional strokes to ensure an ember forms.

The smoke produced should be thick.

Handling the ember: Handle the ember carefully. Tilt the hearth gently, using a twig to secure the ember if necessary. Protect it from moisture and avoid heavy breaths that could blow it away. Allow the ember to consolidate and glow before transferring it to your tinder.

Initially a bow-drill ember is a fragile pile of dust.

After the ember has consolidated, take it the shortest distance possible to your tinder bundle.

Tinder: Dry tinder is critical. Even the best friction fire technique fails with damp tinder. Success requires absolute dryness, since there's no partial success in fire lighting. Many students struggle at this stage until they fully appreciate how vital dry tinder is.

A student rejoices with their first bow-drill success.

Persistence and teamwork: Keep your ego aside. If you are in a situation where you really need a fire (as opposed to practicing), effort without success is simply not enough. If with a partner, collaborate; one operating each end of the bow, both stabilizing the bearing block. Teamwork often turns the tide, even when the conditions are against you.

If there are two people present, don't struggle on your own.

Common reasons why bow drill fails:

- Poor material selection: wrong wood; right wood but too hard or too soft.
- Poor carving: spindle not straight, has oval cross section, is thinner in some places than others, or has too many flat facets; hearth is too thick, too thin or twisted, or won't sit flat on the ground.
- Bow is too heavy.
- Bow is too long or too short.
- Allowing the hearth to move while drilling.
- Not clamping the bearing-block hand firmly enough to your leg.
- Not drilling for long enough.
- Not enough pressure.
- Cordage slips when sufficient pressure is applied (cordage not tight enough).
- Being impatient and not allowing the ember to consolidate, or handling it roughly, resulting in the ember disintegrating when added to the tinder bundle.
- Damp tinder.
- Not enough tinder.
- Not enough contact between ember and tinder.
- Blowing too hard or too softly.
- Wrong attitude!

My final tip: Be positive. As the last point in the above list suggests, the main obstacle to success with bow-drill sets is lack of belief. You must believe you can do it. You should set out with the mindset that success is inevitable. If not, then why try? An ember won't happen by accident. You must make it happen. If you've never achieved an ember on your own, this can be difficult to believe. Then persistence is your key ally. Don't give up! It takes a while to get everything right, but it will come. I struggled with bow drill at first, but once I'd practiced and attained the right mental attitude, it was as if someone had flicked a switch from "hard" to "easy." Eventually, if you practice enough, you will find the same.

CLEARING UP AFTER A FIRE

Leaving minimal trace is a core principle of bushcraft, demonstrating respect for the environment and future visitors. A properly cleared fire site is safe and clean and leaves no visible impact.

Throughout my travels, I've seen many poorly maintained fire sites—usually due to ignorance, though a small minority may not care. For those of us who do, setting a good example by leaving no trace is essential. When done well, it's invisible but impactful, preventing campers, hikers, and bushcraft enthusiasts from gaining a bad reputation.

Why Clearing Up Matters

1. **Safety:** Fires must be fully extinguished to prevent smoldering and potential wildfires. Use ample water to cool visible coals and the ground beneath, especially near coniferous roots.
2. **Environmental impact:** Obvious fire sites encourage repeated use, leading to overuse, vegetation damage, and concentrated camping. This is particularly harmful in fragile ecosystems.
3. **Aesthetics:** Fire remnants disrupt the wilderness experience. Signs of human presence diminish the sense of remoteness and exploration.

In designated camping areas, centralized fire locations help minimize impact. However, even here, leaving trash, half-burned logs, or cluttered fire circles is disrespectful and unhelpful. Proper cleanup demonstrates responsibility and ensures better conditions for future visitors.

How to Clear Up After a Fire

Clearing up a fire site starts with thinking ahead:

- Clear the ground before lighting your fire if needed.
- Consider your fuel requirements—how much and what type you need for cooking, warmth, morale, or as a camp focal point.
- Time your fire to burn out efficiently. Plan so only ashes remain by the time you break camp. If half-burned logs remain, you've overestimated.
- Ensure your fire cleanup task is practical. Water is often necessary to extinguish fires fully, so avoid camping far from a water source.

When cleaning, thoroughly remove all litter, including packaging, foil, and cans. These materials won't decompose and should always be packed out. Carry a trash bag. Flatten cans to save space. Modern packaging, such as foil-lined sachets, often leaves residue when burned, so inspect and clear these remnants.

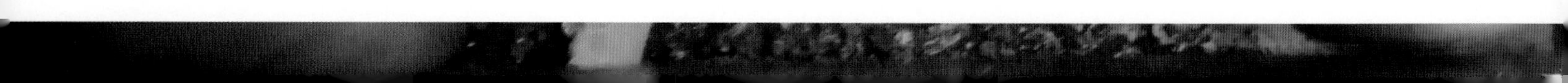

Finally, check that the ground beneath the fire is cool to the touch, especially in areas with tree roots or peat. Scatter any remaining ash to disperse traces of your fire and restore the site as closely as possible to its original state.

For many, campfires are fundamental to outdoor experiences, but those who light one must do so responsibly. It's crucial to understand how to safely and cleanly manage a fire site, ensuring you leave the campsite, including the fire area, as you'd hope to find it.

3. *The ground underneath the campfire can harden. Break it up with a pointed stick. Then add more water so it can seep into the ground.*

1. *Think ahead. Let your campfire burn down so you don't have lots of half-burned wood to deal with.*

4. *Carefully check that everything is cool.*

2. *Add plenty of water to douse the embers.*

5. *Get your hands right in to check that the ground underneath is cool.*

6. *Picking up the cold, damp charcoal from the campfire.*

9. *Cover up the campfire site with the material you cleared when preparing the site of your campfire.*

7. *Distribute the cold, wet ashes from your campfire.*

The center of this picture is the site of a campfire. A good cleanup job makes it very hard to detect.

8. *Remove all wet charcoal until only damp earth remains.*

The author standing next to the site of his campfire.

Strong foundations build confidence with fire. Here, a student during one of my Elementary Wilderness Bushcraft courses succeeds with the challenge to light a fire with feathersticks, using only one match.

Sheltercraft

Shelter is a key component of protecting ourselves from environmental conditions that are demanding on our physiology and could do us real harm. From a more general outdoor-living perspective, shelter allows us to live in the bush more comfortably. It allows us to enjoy sufficient rest each evening and not waste precious calories or, for that matter, precious time. Particularly if we're on a journey, moving each day, needing most of the day's time for traveling, and setting up camp in the evening, we want to be quick and efficient with our shelter setups.

Sometimes we'll need shelter to keep off the worst of the day's heat, or purely to prevent us and our gear from being drenched, even though it might be warm enough not to induce hypothermia. In other circumstances, shelter might be as much about keeping biting insects at bay as keeping us protected from the environmental conditions. Much of the time, though, your sheltercraft will be aimed at keeping you warm in an otherwise cool environment.

MECHANISMS OF HEAT TRANSFER

Your body needs to maintain a core temperature of 98.6°F (37°C). If you lose more heat than you generate, your core temperature will fall. If this heat loss is not arrested, you will succumb to hypothermia. If you generate more heat than you can dissipate, or if you are absorbing heat from the environment, then your core temperature will rise. If this heat gain is not arrested, you will succumb to hyperthermia. Both hypothermia and hyperthermia are potentially fatal and pose serious risks to the outdoors person. Understanding the mechanisms of heat transfer helps you better manage your temperature, remaining comfortable and safe. This is particularly relevant to the positioning and erecting of shelters.

There are five possible mechanisms of heat transfer with the environment: convection, conduction, evaporation, respiration, and radiation. Convection, conduction, and evaporation are the main mechanisms that cause excessive heat loss when we are trying to stay warm in a cool environment.

Heat loss through **convection** occurs when a surface is in contact with a moving fluid or gas, such as the air surrounding our bodies. The air closest to our skin is heated by our bodies, but if it moves away, colder air will take its place, resulting in heat loss. To stay warm, we need to trap warm air near our bodies, which is achieved by using appropriate insulation and windproof materials. Conversely, you can use a breeze to help cool off in hot temperatures.

Heat loss through **conduction** occurs when we come into direct contact with cold surfaces or objects. Heat is transmitted faster to metals with higher conductivity. To reduce conductive heat loss, we need to insulate our bodies from cold surfaces with poor heat conductors, such as sleeping mats or natural materials.

Evaporation is a highly effective heat loss mechanism. When a liquid turns to vapor or gas, it requires a lot of energy, which can come from our body heat. This is why sweating is so effective in keeping us cool on hot days. In cold environments, however, evaporation can be very detrimental to us. In the context of sleeping and shelter construction, we need to prevent environmental moisture, such as rain, sleet, and dew, from entering our clothing or bedding. Also, we should avoid sweating inside our sleep systems or breathing moisture into them. Conversely, in hot climates, if air is so humid that sweat does not evaporate from our skin, then we are at great risk of overheating unless we moderate our activity.

Heat loss through **radiation** occurs when heat radiates from our bodies to a surrounding cool environment. The wider the temperature differential between you and the environment, the more heat energy you will radiate. Even so, under most circumstances this mechanism of heat loss is not as significant as convection, conduction, and evaporation. But the actions taken to minimize these three generally will also help reduce heat loss through radiation. Conversely, in cold conditions we can benefit from radiation from a fire or from the sun. But in hot conditions, we may need to protect ourselves from the sun's radiation to avoid hyperthermia.

Respiration is the process of breathing, which also results in heat loss. As we inhale cold air, it is warmed before reaching our lungs. Then we breathe out warmed air, resulting in some heat loss. In the context of shelters, we can reduce heat loss through breathing by raising the temperature of the air inside. But remember you shouldn't breathe into your sleeping bag, since this will add a detrimental amount of moisture.

The author in the Norwegian mountains. Strong winds and low temperatures can create the potential for massive convective heat loss.

SHELTER PRINCIPLES

When it comes to effective shelters for outdoor living, there are a range of principles that are commonly applied to various environments.

These principles ensure adequate protection from the elements. For cooler environments, one of the primary principles to consider is trapping air inside the shelter space. This can be achieved by constructing an enclosed leaf hut, a quinzee (snow shelter), or a mountain tent. Another approach, sometimes employed in combination, is to trap air in the shelter's construction material, such as leaf litter or snow. Erecting a shelter with a sufficiently steep roof, walls, or sides, along with sufficiently thick thatching material, prevents water ingress from rain. In very cold environments, a cold well for cold air to drop below the living space can be included in snow shelters or tent vestibules.

Alternatively, having a more open shelter with a sizable fire in front of the shelter can provide active heating for the interior and occupant(s). Examples include an open-fronted debris shelter, the classic northern forest lean-to shelter, or a tarp set at a single angle with a fire in front. A more enclosed shelter with a fire for warmth but sufficient ventilation to avoid smoke inhalation or carbon monoxide poisoning is another option. Examples of such shelters include a lavvu or kota with an open fire, a heated canvas tent with a wood-burning stove and chimney, a group shelter of natural materials with a fire inside, and an igloo with a kudlik (oil lamp) burning seal fat.

Using an insulated sleeping pad or creating an insulated mattress, bough bed, or raised bed can help reduce the conduction of heat into the ground or snow beneath. Using some form of mat, skin, duvet, blanket, or sleeping bag to hold air directly over or around the sleeper has been employed in innumerable modes of shelter living; it is a well-understood and highly effective means of conserving body heat.

For warmer environments, having open sides to a shelter to allow airflow is a commonly used principle. This includes mesh netting in tents to ensure adequate ventilation. A roof is necessary to keep the sun at bay. By placing the shelter under the shade of trees, the heat of the sun can be further reduced. Roofs can also be used to repel tropical downpours. Unless smoke is needed to prevent insects from spreading, fires are often kept at some distance from people to avoid overheating. Raised beds or platforms can similarly be used to increase airflow, stay off wet ground, and remain elevated above creatures such as ants, snakes, or spiders. Hammocks are another popular option in warmer environments.

SHELTER PLACEMENT

Choosing a suitable site for your shelter is crucial to your comfort and safety outdoors. Whether you're building a natural shelter or using a tent or tarp, there are some key considerations to remember:

1. **Aspect:** It's worthwhile considering the prevailing wind direction and sun exposure when choosing a site for a shelter. You want to position the shelter to block the wind and provide shade when necessary. Sometimes, particularly in cold conditions, you should seek sun exposure.
2. **Lay of the land:** Unless you are seeking respite from biting insects, avoid placing your shelter on exposed high points, since they can be windy and uncomfortably cool. Also, steer clear of localized cold pockets, such as dips or small valleys, where cold air accumulates. Be sure to choose a site with proper drainage to prevent flooding. Avoid camping on dried-up riverbeds, since they can quickly become flood zones during heavy rain.
3. **Ground conditions:** Choose a flat, level spot for your shelter, avoiding rocks, roots, and boggy ground. This will ensure a comfortable sleeping surface and prevent damage to your gear.
4. **Resources:** Choose a site with an adequate water source. If you plan to build a fire, make sure there are the resources you need, and a safe place to site your fire. For natural shelters, look for a site with nearby building materials such as branches, leaves, and boughs.
5. **Insects and wildlife:** Avoid setting up camp in spots that seem to have activity of wasps, hornets, bees, or ants significantly above the baseline for the area. There's probably a nest nearby. Mosquitoes can be inescapable, but it's advisable to avoid spots close to standing water and that have no breeze. Be mindful of animal trails and signs of animal activity.
6. **Environmental hazards:** Be aware of potential hazards such as dangerous trees, widowmakers, steep slopes, or areas prone to rockfalls. Avoid camping near these hazards to ensure your safety.
7. **Environmental sensitivity:** Choose a site that minimizes environmental impact and doesn't disrupt natural habitats. Avoid camping in sensitive areas or with fragile plant life.

By considering these factors, you can find the ideal site for your shelter that provides comfort, safety, and minimal impact on the environment.

TARP SETUPS

Tarps are highly versatile, ideal for forest and bush camping. Traditional canvas tarps serve communal base camps well, while modern materials offer personal tarps ranging from military bashas to lightweight silicon nylon. These tarps are compact for easy packing. Budget options include inexpensive garden tarps.

Inexpensive garden tarp.

Personal tarps allow flexible camping setups, even in treeless areas with trekking poles. With basic knots, they're quick to set up, perfect for itinerant bivvy camping. Tarps work well on the ground with a bivvy bag for added moisture and wind protection. For bug protection, suspend a net underneath or pair it with a hammock for an elevated sleep.

Lightweight silicone nylon tarp in northern Sweden.

Tarp with mosquito net in Australia.

Tarp and hammock setup.

Tarps offer adaptable shelter solutions, often balancing protection and ventilation better than traditional tents.

Tarp Knots

There is no one definitive set of knots that must be used to suspend a tarp and position the guylines. But you should know some that allow you to set up your tarp tidily and quickly. The following knots are useful to know. Furthermore, they all are tied in a way that makes them quick-release. Quick setups are always beneficial, especially in poor weather. Fast takedowns are especially valuable on a journey when you need to make distance between camps.

A tidy tarp setup is enabled by good knots.

Evenk Hitch

This is a nifty way of tying a slipped figure-eight knot with a quick-release. You can use it to attach your tarp ridgeline to a tree. Tie this first.

1. *Take the cord around a tree and bring it over your nondominant hand.*

2. *Wrap the cord around your hand. Note that the palm is up.*

3. *Keeping hold of the live end, begin to drop your fingers toward the ground.*

4. *Rotate your wrist so that your fingers begin to rise again (on the opposite side of the ridgeline to where they started).*

5. *Continue to rotate your wrist to bring your fingers above the standing part of the cord.*

6. *Complete the rotation so your hand ends up over the standing part, palm down.*

7. *Grab the live end between your fingers.*

8. *Pull a bight of the live end through the loop.*

9. *Pull the bight while holding the live end with your other hand to keep it from pulling through the loop. The knot should now have a figure-eight shape.*

10. Pull back to tighten the figure-eight shape of the knot.

11. Slide the knot up to the tree and cinch it there.

12. Completed knot. Pulling the end will release it.

Taut Tarp Hitch

This is the second knot to tie on your ridgeline. Unlike the Evenk hitch, it can be tensioned, giving you a nice straight ridgeline, or pulling your tarp tight, if it does not have a separate ridgeline. If there is a trick to this knot, it's maintaining tension in the line as you pass it from one hand to the other as you form the knot.

1. *Take the cord around a second tree and pull it tight.*

2. *Keeping the tension in place, take the live end over the standing part.*

3. *Bring the live end back under the standing part.*

4. *Cross the live end over to the top.*

5. *Take the line back around the tree.*

6. *Keeping the live end on top, bring it across the top of the ridgeline, creating a triangle shape.*

7. *Bring a bight up through the triangle shape.*

8. *Note the size and position of the bight.*

9. *Pass your fingers through to grab the live end.*

10. *Pull a second bight through the first. This locks off the knot and leaves it quick-release.*

Adjustable Guyline Hitch

Sometimes called a slippery adjustable loop, this knot allows you to create a sliding knot to tension your guylines that will stay in place. It is related to other knots such as prusiks (see page 121) and is closely related to the tautline hitch. Start by bringing the guyline down from your tarp, around the peg or other fixed point you are using to tie out, then return the line back up toward the tarp.

1. *Take the live end across the standing part.*

2. *Take the live end around the standing part, then up through the middle of the loop created.*

3. *Pull the live end through and you should have a wrap of cord around the standing part.*

4. *Do the same again by passing the live end up through the space between the two lines.*

5. *Make another wrap below the first wrap.*

6. *Make a third turn, but this time, instead of coming up through the middle, go around both sections of line that run down to the peg.*

7. *Pull a bight through the loop you have created. (We pull a bight through rather than the whole live end so that the knot will be quick-release.)*

8. *Pull the third wrap tight to consolidate the structure of the knot.*

9. *To tighten the guyline, pull the standing part away from the tarp and the knot toward it.*

Pitching Your Tarp

1. Choose a suitably spaced pair of trees between which you want to suspend your tarp.
2. Check for overhead hazards such as widowmakers before setting up the tarp.
3. Use the Evenk hitch to tie the ridgeline to the first of the two trees.
4. Use the taut tarp hitch to tension and attach the ridgeline to the second tree.
5. If your tarp has prusiks attached, pull out the tarp and position it by using the prusiks.
6. Pull out a guyline at an angle that bisects the corner angle of the tarp.
7. Place a peg at a distance from the tarp that gives you the desired angle of the tarp sheet.
8. Tie the guyline to the peg, using an adjustable guyline hitch.
9. Repeat steps 6–7 for each corner.
10. If desired, tie a line under the apex of your tarp as a hanging line.
11. If you will sleep on the ground, clear the ground under the tarp of thorns or debris.
12. Set up your sleeping system if it is not already in place.

Using a Hanging Line

Maintain organization with a hanging line tied under the apex. Use it to store equipment and clothing within reach, and even to air out your sleeping bag during the day. Attach lanyards or the headbands of headlamps with a lark's foot or girth hitch (see page 121).

Items neatly organized on a hanging line under a tarp.

Sleeping bag airing on a hanging line.

Additional Tarp-Pitching Ideas

Consider an open-fronted lean-to setup with a fire for warmth. For more protection, large tarps can be pegged to the ground like an open-ended tent, and smaller ones with press studs (snap fasteners), such as hootchies, can join together for a larger cover.

Two smaller tarps combined and pegged to the ground.

Enhance this style with an A-frame stick structure, ensuring no sharp ends damage the tarp. You can fill shelter ends with natural materials for extra insulation and space, especially in colder weather conditions. This versatile approach can provide shelter for up to four people using a tarp area that would normally protect only two.

A-frame shelters with tarp coverings and enclosed ends.

IMPROVISED SHELTERS

Shelters come in many forms, from natural formations such as caves or rock overhangs to constructed shelters requiring more effort.

A natural rockshelter with dried vegetation added to provide comfort.

Shelters serve purposes beyond warmth. In some places, they shield against sun exposure and maintain coolness. In others, even in warm air temperatures, they protect from heavy rain.

This shelter in northern Australia provides shade.

Shelters fall into two broad categories: open sided or enclosed. They can also be classified by their dependence on fire for warmth. Often, fire is the critical factor for comfort. In extreme cold, such as a forest at -4°F (-20°C), a large fire can sustain you through the night, with shelter playing a secondary role.

A long-log fire with no shelter at -4 °F (-20 °C).

Bedding

Regardless of the shelter type, insulation from the ground is essential. Conductive heat loss is significant, even in warm environments. Bedding should be comfortable for prolonged use, requiring matting, boughs, or a springy platform.

A raised log bed, covered in springy twigs for additional comfort.

A comfy bed of tea-tree foliage in Australia.

This winter bivouac site in Canada has been lined with spruce and fir boughs for insulation.

Improvised Arctic forest shelter in Scandinavia, with a thick mattress of spruce boughs.

A Range of Options

Shelter approaches are not limited to survival vs. camping. Natural shelters can complement modern gear. For example, you might combine a natural shelter with a sleeping bag or wool blanket. You might decide to hike light into an area, bivvying along the way, then build a shelter for a fixed camp so you can operate in an area for a while.

Natural shelter using modern sleeping gear.

Day hikers, often unprepared for overnight stays, can use emergency items such as plastic bags as improvised tarps or bedding. Stuffing one bag with leaves creates a mattress, and layering two bags with insulation in between forms a makeshift sleeping bag.

Polyethylene bag cut open and strung as a tarp.

Polyethylene bag stuffed with springy vegetation to form a mattress.

Poly bag tarp and mattress combined.

Brightly colored sheets attract attention while sheltering.

Environmental Considerations

Building natural shelters requires environmental awareness. Overharvesting materials disrupts ecosystems, while constructing in fragile habitats causes long-term damage. You must consider the impact on other outdoor users. This includes avoiding overly diminishing resources others might want, or need, to use, such as firewood. There is also an aesthetic consideration to leaving an area as you want to find it. Additionally, you should check the rules for shelter building on the land you intend to access. These might not be rules governing shelter building explicitly but more general restrictions on cutting green foliage or even cutting dead standing wood. By being mindful of your ethical responsibilities and minimizing your impact, you can enjoy natural shelters when appropriate. If you genuinely need a shelter, however, to guard against you, or your companions, dying of exposure, you should build a shelter regardless.

Tools for Shelter Construction

Natural shelters can often be built without tools, using snapped branches for framework. However, tools such as folding saws or belt knives significantly improve efficiency. Axes, machetes, or parangs are invaluable in specific environments for cutting larger or denser materials. Snow shelters benefit from snow shovels or improvised tools such as snowshoe scoops.

Enclosed Shelters (Without Fire)

Closed Debris Huts

These fully enclosed shelters trap warm air and protect against wind and rain without requiring fire. Frameworks are built from sturdy branches, ribbed with smaller sticks, and covered with insulating debris. Interlocking branches often negate the need for cordage. Their natural camouflage can make them hard to locate, even unintentionally.

Thermal A-Frame Shelters

Compact and efficient, these shelters are constructed with a single long pole supported by a log or interlocking Y-sticks. Covered in natural insulation such as leaves or moss, they are quick to build and ideal for emergencies.

Two-Person Debris Shelters

These low-profile shelters trap heat efficiently for two occupants. Thermal shelters must be sized appropriately based on their users. These shelters are constructed using an upright Y-pole and two extended poles on either side. These poles act as crossbeams, creating a double thermal A-frame in the foot pockets. The long beams are laid apart so there is space for a doorway between them. The bottom of the Y should be just above the occupants' heads while sitting. The two long beams should be long enough that, with the ends laid in the Y-pole, the occupants can lie underneath them.

Two-person debris shelter.

Creating the structure of a two-person debris hut.

Gathering armfuls of leaves to cover the hut.

The structural components should be strong enough to hold the weight of the materials piled upon them without the shelter collapsing. Once you have a sturdy frame of these three components, sticks are laid up against the frame as rafters. These should be laid next to each other such that there are minimal gaps between them to stop the thatching material from falling through. It's essential that stick ends don't protrude above the overall structure. Otherwise, rainwater will run down the sticks and into the shelter. The shelter is then covered with leaf litter. You should ensure this thatching material is thick enough to provide adequate insulation and protection from the rain. With leaf litter, this equates to making the covering as deep as the distance from your hand to your armpit.

Snow Shelters

Snow in forests remains powdery and must be compacted to build shelters. A quinzee, made by hollowing out a hardened snow mound, provides insulation, maintaining temperatures just below freezing. Simple tunnel designs suffice for individuals. A larger quinzee with a sleeping platform is more comfortable for groups. Adding a cold well enhances comfort.

A cold well can be created by digging into the mound low down, then digging upward to create a T-shaped hollow. The sleeping platforms will be either side of the trench, at the top of the T shape. Alternatively, dig an almost circular platform with a segment dropped lower, nearest the door. Cold wells can also be used in tent vestibules when winter camping on a snow platform.

Building a quinzee in Ontario.

Digging into deep windslab in Norwegian mountains.

Digging out a quinzee.

A cold well has been dug in this tent vestibule.

Open Shelters

Free-standing, open-fronted shelters seem universal. They are easy to construct and can be made from a variety of natural materials. Find the most naturally sheltered spot—any breeze will diminish your shelter's effectiveness. Look out for the opportunity to gain protection from any screens of small trees and overhead branches of larger trees.

If you want to have a fire in front of an open-fronted shelter, the orientation relative to any breeze or wind is critical. There is a common misconception that putting the shelter back to the wind is beneficial. While it is beneficial as a windbreak, there will also be an eddy effect. Air will pass up and over the shelter, then recirculate in the opposite direction. If the back of the shelter is to the wind, the recirculation of air—and smoke from the fire it picks up—is straight back into the shelter. This is very unpleasant for the shelter occupant. Thus, it is much better to have the front of the shelter parallel to any breeze, so it blows the smoke away from you sideways.

In cool conditions, it's beneficial to orientate the shelter so that the open side is in the sun during the day. Assuming you are living and working out of the shelter, this will contribute to your warmth during the day. If you can get the sun for only part of the day, given the other constraints such as wind direction, getting the sun on to you and your shelter in the morning will make the most difference.

Open-Fronted Debris Hut

This shelter combines a weatherproof structure with the warmth of a fire outside its open side. Its framework relies on interlocked sticks, covered with leaf litter or larger natural materials such as sheets of bark. When used by pairs, positioning shelters opposite each other, either side of a central fire, enhances efficiency.

Debris hut with palm leaf covering.

Lattice framework lashed with natural materials.

Shelter covered largely with grasses and bracken, with comfy bed of springy shrub branches.

Debris hut with leaf litter covering.

A thick, insulating covering of leaf litter on the rear of this open-fronted debris hut.

Two open-fronted shelters sharing a fire.

Boreal Forest Lean-To Shelters

These long-lasting shelters suit colder climates and repeated use justifies the time and effort required to build them. They are not a quick overnight shelter.

Lean-to shelter with raised bed and spruce bedding in Sweden.

Revisiting a lean-to built in a previous winter.

Positioning and orientation are vital when building a boreal lean-to. Avoid low points where cold air gathers and select a site with ample materials nearby. To construct, locate two sturdy trees spaced to accommodate the shelter. Cut a strong green-wood crossbeam and lash it between the trees. If cordage is unavailable, prop the crossbeam with solid Y-poles at the front. Position the crossbeam between the back wall of the shelter and the upright trees to ensure the structure's weight keeps it secure.

The back and sides of a lean-to shelter thatched with spruce boughs.

The crossbeam's height should align with the combined dimensions of the bed and the desired 50–60-degree back wall angle. The bed must be wide enough to lie comfortably. Attach angled poles to form the back wall and strip them of branches, using the cut material for thatching and bedding. Trim poles to size as needed, using excess for the raised bed platform.

Lay poles tightly together for the back wall, or space them a hand span apart—a balance of efficiency and material use. The bed platform should consist of poles strong enough to support your weight, with slight flexibility for comfort. Alternate thicker and thinner ends of tapered poles to create an even surface. Cover the platform with boughs for insulation and comfort.

The fire should run parallel to the shelter, at least as long as the occupant's height. Position it close enough to warm the shelter's back wall while radiating heat directly to your body. Leave just enough space to sit on the bed and extend your legs near the fire.

Lean-to with parallel long-log fire in front.

If available, use large dead-standing timber for a long-log fire. Stack two logs at the base with one on top, stabilizing the structure with greenwood stakes hammered diagonally to form an X shape at each end. This setup ensures consistent flames and heat. Alternatively, construct a long fire with smaller-diameter deadwood.

Group Shelters

Group shelters accommodate multiple occupants, combining individual structures or creating tipi-like frameworks. Central fires enable warmth, cooking, and drying clothes. They can provide a space to work and rest too.

Five-person group shelter with cooking space.

Large lean-to group shelter with side-by-side sleeping.

Adjust Your Expectations About Sleep

If you are sleeping inside a closed debris hut with warm sleeping gear inside its dark and soundproofed interior, you might have the most peaceful sleep of your life. For other permutations of sleeping inside natural shelters, you would do well to adjust your expectations, as well as to discard common misconceptions.

If you rely on fire to stay warm overnight, excessive clothing or sleeping gear will insulate you against fire heat. You may feel warmer by opening your clothing or putting it over you, rather than on your person. For example, if you have a long overcoat, you can use it as a blanket. Personally, I sleep best on my side, with my front facing the fire. Therefore, I tend to keep wearing the overcoat but have it open at the front—this means my back is kept covered and warm while my front gets the benefit of the fire.

There is a common myth that you will not wake up if you get too cold. I can assure you that as soon as the fire dies down a bit and you feel the chill of the night, you will be awake. As a fire dies down, it also tends to produce more smoke, which, if it comes your way, will also likely wake you up. Once you are awake, the job is to adjust the fire so that it regains the warmth required for you to fall back asleep. Make sure you have plenty of wood ready before dark. You'll burn more wood than you expect during a night. So, you will sleep, but it will be in shorter stretches than you are used to. Until you get used to this routine, you will likely feel tired the next morning.

Even though a fire will keep you warm, you have to adjust to sleeping for shorter periods than you do in a sleeping bag or at home.

Water Procurement and Processing

Humans need to drink water regularly. In most environments we suffer a significant depletion of physiological and mental function after only a day or two of no consumption of water. In hot environments, or when our physical work rate is high, with increased usage of the body's water for perspiration, serious dehydration can occur within hours.

Water is heavy, however, weighing 2.1 lbs. per quart (1 kg per liter). So, for most self-propelled journeys that are longer than a day, you can't carry enough drinking water for your trip; you will have to source drinking water along the way. For multiday trips, you will also need water for cooking. Even if you are hiking into the woods for a long weekend at a fixed camp, packing in all the water you need for drinking, cooking, washing dishes and hygiene, along with your gear and food, is going to be challenging.

So, if you are going to spend any time out in natural environments, you need to understand how to source water. This will be harder in some environments or seasons than others. But the more you understand about the environment, water indicators, and methods of collection, the better your chances will be.

You also need an understanding of what might be wrong with any water once you have found a source. You need to understand what potential contaminants there might be, including pathogenic organisms.

Once you understand what contaminants might be in your water sources, you need to understand the different ways of dealing with the contaminants. Critically, you need to know which purification techniques deal with which contaminants—because there is no single method that solves all potential problems.

Once you understand which techniques of purification work on which contaminants, you need to develop or follow established protocols that will reliably deal with all the contaminants that might be in your water source. This usually involves the combination of several techniques.

But more than just picking one protocol we like the look of and then sticking with it in any scenario, we need to have a good understanding of alternative protocols, which are optimal for different circumstances, since there are pros and cons to each, even though they all work.

You then need to apply the reliable protocols in a robust way. You need to maintain a failsafe system, even if you are on your own. Do not cut corners. It's even more important when working as a group. Everyone needs to know what the system is and follow it for the benefit of the group. If one person compromises the group's water supply, then everyone is at risk of becoming ill.

Even if water looks crystal clear, you can't necessarily trust it. You should have a good knowledge of water purification protocols in order to provide the hydration you need.

DRINKING ENOUGH WATER

Many survival texts will tell you a lack of water intake over several days can lead to death, especially in hot climates. Certainly, you should not underestimate how quickly you can become a victim of dehydration and heat-related illnesses in hot environments.

More generally, however, you should understand how dehydration will affect you long before you get close to being dead. This will help you recognize incipient dehydration, then reverse it before it becomes more serious, but also optimize your time outdoors.

Even a small degree of dehydration can negatively affect your physical performance, mental acuity, motivation, and mood. In the context of outdoor life, all of these could have detrimental knock-on effects, reducing your ability to complete a journey, organize a camp, make good navigational decisions, keep yourself safe from objective hazards, or simply get along with companions.

Early symptoms of dehydration vary in intensity and order of appearance in each of us. But generally, dehydration starts to make people feel thirsty, fatigued, indecisive, irritable, and impatient. Headaches are common, some feel lightheaded, and some report tingly fingers and toes. Following this, probably with a greater level of dehydration, people report muscle aches and pains and nausea, and a greater number report feeling lightheaded.

You should also bear in mind that some symptoms of dehydration cross over with the effects of extended exertion (e.g., fatigue), and low blood sugar (e.g., irritability). Also, if you normally drink lots of caffeinated drinks during the day, switching to largely water on a hiking trip, for example, may increase your chances of headaches due to caffeine withdrawal. Regardless, you should endeavor to stay well hydrated. Being dehydrated will only ever make you feel worse.

It would be a mistake to think of dehydration as associated only with warm, dry environments. Dehydration can be an issue in any environment. The human body loses water through perspiration, respiration, urination, and normal defecation. Furthermore, diarrhea or vomiting can result in significant additional water loss. If you do not drink enough water to replace lost water, then you will become dehydrated.

Increased environmental temperature, increased exertion, or both will lead to increased perspiration, which will increase your demand for water. As a guide, moderate outdoor activity in the warmer months of temperate climates will require you to drink around 1 gallon (3.75 liters) of water per day to stay well hydrated. In hot climates you will need to drink more, perhaps a quarter of a gallon per hour of activity, which could amount to 3 gallons (11 liters) per day.

In cold climates that are significantly below freezing, where the air is literally freeze dried, your water loss can increase compared to a cool temperate climate. Even though you should be trying to avoid sweating, so your clothing does not become damp, imperceptible perspiration can still increase due to the dryness of the air. Inhaling dry air (and exhaling moist air) will also result in losing more moisture than breathing in humid air. Hence, in cold, dry environments, you may also need to increase your water intake. In addition to all the usual benefits of good levels of hydration, in a very cold environment good hydration helps maintain good circulation, which helps prevent cold injuries.

Obtaining drinkable water outdoors is rarely as easy as turning on a tap at home. Moreover, many don't habitually drink sufficient water at home or at work, resulting in being continually dehydrated to some degree. In addition, a lot of drinks are laced with caffeine, sugar, or both. Chronic suboptimal hydration might not be so noticeable for sedentary folk in climate-controlled spaces such as offices, homes, and vehicles. Transfer the same poor habits outdoors, however, and they can have immediate effects. Most of us need to make a conscious effort to drink enough water to support our activities outdoors.

So, how do we ensure we drink enough water?

Maintaining good hydration is a daily effort. One of the best things you can do for your hydration each day is to drink plenty in the morning. Wherever you are, drink at least a quart (1 liter) of water immediately after rising. This is partly because you will not have drunk anything significant for at least eight hours beforehand. Drinking plenty first thing helps you get ahead with your day's hydration efforts.

In the context of wilderness journeys, another key hydration juncture is when you stop to make camp for the evening. Get your water production system(s) up and running as soon as possible and hydrate early, preferably before eating your evening meal. The sooner you can rehydrate after the day's efforts, the better, giving your body time to assimilate the water it needs before the end of the day. Plus, if you leave your rehydration efforts until shortly before bed, the thought of having to get up in the night to urinate might be enough to dissuade you from rehydrating properly. Start getting water down as soon as you can after arriving at your camp spot.

During the day, take proper drinks from the water you are carrying, don't merely sip it. When you stop to drink, you should aim to drink 5–8½ fl. oz (150–250 ml), rather than sipping tiny amounts. Don't wait until you feel thirsty to start drinking. Thirst is a poor indicator. You will already be somewhat dehydrated before you feel particularly thirsty.

Not having enough capacity in your water bottles can mean you are inevitably going to be prone to dehydration. Before you even leave home, think about what your water situation will be on your trip. How far apart will water sources be? How much water should you be consuming? How much carrying capacity do you need during the day to last you between opportunities to refill your bottles or water bladders?

When you come to a water source, make full use of it. Don't just refill your bottles and move on. Refill bottles and drink your fill while you are there, then top off or refill your bottles again, then move on. Later in this chapter we'll look at means of making water safe to drink. Some are quicker to deploy than others. Some are more practical in some environments than others. What you carry with you to produce safe drinking water during the day should also be considered in the context of the environment and your mode of travel. Not having convenient, efficient systems for water purification during the day could lead to you not drinking enough water, even if there is plenty of it about.

As well as monitoring how you feel, checking for symptoms of dehydration such as thirst and headache, you should also monitor yourself for outward signs of dehydration such as dry lips or a dry mouth. An important marker to monitor is your urine output. Generally, you should be producing at least a quart (1 liter) of straw-colored urine per day. Any less than this, or if your urine is significantly darker, it is a sign of dehydration.

LOCATING AND COLLECTING WATER

Surface water, such as streams, rivers, lakes, and ponds, is often the most accessible water source. However, it may be scarce in some environments or during specific seasons. Understanding the environment and seasonal patterns significantly improves your chances of finding water.

In some environments, or seasons, surface water can be hard to find. Serengeti, Tanzania.

Reading the Landscape

Water naturally flows downhill, collecting in low spots or channels. Look for hollows, depressions, narrow canyons, cliff bases, bends in dry riverbeds, and rock kettles. Even if dry, such locations may still harbor damp soil or small pools beneath the surface.

Vegetation can be a reliable indicator of water. Trees such as willows (*Salix*), alders (*Alnus*), poplars, and cottonwoods (*Populus*) thrive near consistent water sources. Similarly, plants such as soft rush (*Juncus effusus*) favor locally damp ground.

Willows and alders favor areas of consistently wet ground.

*Plants such as soft rush (*Juncus effusus*) indicate damp ground.*

Clues from Wildlife

Observing wildlife behaviors can lead you to water sources.

- Insects: Hornets, bees, and butterflies are often found near water.
- Birds: Seed-eating birds typically rely on water, while flocks may congregate around water sources. Look for the direction they are flying.
- Animal trails: Converging animal trails often lead to water.
- Larger animals: Species such as cape buffalo depend on waterholes for survival.

Cape buffalo rely on waterholes. (Amanda Quaine)

Converging game trails, South Africa.

Finding Water in Arid Landscapes

In dry regions, springs, seeps, and riparian zones are key water sources. Look for green vegetation, especially larger plants, since these indicate the presence of underground or surface water. Dry riverbeds may still contain water under shaded bends or undercut banks. Use binoculars to scout vegetation or possible water sources more efficiently. Human-made structures such as windmills, cattle tanks, and abandoned homesteads can also indicate wells or water supplies. Always purify such water before drinking.

This spring is a reliable water source. East Sussex, UK.

Large trees such as cottonwoods suggest water. Arizona, USA.

A dry watercourse in the South African bush might still harbor water.

Digging for Water

When the ground appears damp, dig a hole to allow water to seep in. Here's how:

1. **Choose a location:** Look for damp soil, dry riverbeds, or depressions where water may collect.
2. **Dig a hole:** Use a shovel or digging stick to create a hole with clean sides. The deeper the hole, the more water is likely to seep in.
3. **Let water collect:** Allow water to seep in and pool at the bottom.
4. **Remove the first fill:** Discard the initial muddy water, allowing clearer water to replace it.
5. **Prefilter:** Use cloth or a filter bag to filter sediment before purifying the water for drinking.

Dug hole filled with water from the soil.

Damp soil under a dry riverbed in Tanzania.

Hadza man chewing an African baobab branch for water. (Amanda Quaine)

Water from Vegetation

As well as various plants and trees being an indicator of ground water, some species can provide water directly. Examples include collecting fluid directly from some vines, tree saplings, and branches. In any environment where this might be the case, however, you need to have good knowledge of the local flora, in terms of knowing which species may yield water and how to differentiate them from other, possibly toxic species. There may also be specific techniques needed for the sample to yield water.

Drinking water from the five-leaved native grapevine, Cissus hypoglauca. *Australia.*

Transpiration Bags

A widely applicable technique of obtaining water from vegetation in warm climates is the transpiration bag. This requires a plastic bag and a suitable nontoxic tree or shrub. The bag is placed around a sapling or a branch of a tree with healthy foliage and left in direct sunlight. The tree will transpire, releasing moisture into the bag, which will eventually condense and collect in the bottom corner of the bag. Transpiration bags obtain water from vegetation passively. This method requires virtually no energy expense on your part, and nature does all the work. The bag used for this method should be large, clear, without pleats, and reasonably robust. The bag is tied tightly around the branch, creating a greenhouse effect. Transpiration bags work best in strong, direct sunlight. If it is overcast, the bag will not work as effectively.

Follow these steps:

1. **Select the vegetation:** Choose a healthy, leafy specimen of a nontoxic, thornless species, positioned such that it will receive unobstructed sunlight during the collection period.
2. **Position the bag:** Place a clear plastic bag over the branch, ensuring it fully encloses the leaves.
3. **Seal the bag:** Secure the bag tightly at the branch base with cordage to prevent air escape.
4. **Place in sunlight:** Position the branch so it receives maximum sunlight to encourage condensation.
5. **Collect water:** Water will pool at the lowest point of the bag. To drain the water into a container, puncture a small hole in the bottom corner. Reseal the bag by tying off with cordage for continued use.

This method can easily yield around 18 fl. oz. (550 ml) of water daily, sometimes over a quart (1 liter), depending on conditions.

Transpiration bag in use in Australia.

Finding Water in Cold or Wet Environments

Melting Snow

In cold environments, all water might be frozen, or under a thick layer of ice. Then your options for obtaining water are melting snow or making a hole in the ice. Holes can be made with an ice chisel, an ice auger, or even an axe. If the ice is very thick, this can be a lot of work. If there are only a couple of you in your group, staying for one night before moving on, it might be quicker and easier to melt snow. If there are a dozen of you and you are staying for a few days, it could be well worth the effort of cutting through the ice to extract many gallons of water. A further consideration is that water from melted snow can be drunk directly. In contrast, fresh water from a pond or lake might need sterilization before consumption.

To melt snow, you need a heat source. A metal pot can be placed directly over a fire or on a stove, with snow added to the container. Start with a relatively small amount of snow and allow it to melt. This is preferable to filling the pot entirely with snow, since snow nearest the bottom will melt, then soak upward into the snow above, creating an insulating air gap between the bottom of the pot and the air above. This significantly slows the melting process. The pot might also be damaged, depending on its material. Better to melt a small amount of snow first, produce some warm water, then add more snow to it. This snow will melt into the water.

If you do not have a metal pot, you can still melt snow to produce drinking water. The two methods here provide options in various circumstances. The assumption is that you are lightly equipped without shelter or cooking equipment (otherwise you'd be using a metal pot, either on a fire or a stove), but you can light a fire.

The first method, known as a **Finnish marshmallow**, requires a stout pole and compacted snow. Impale a solid lump of compacted snow onto the stick. This is placed near the fire, not over it. The radiant heat melts the snow. Initially, water will soak into the block. However, once saturated, water drips out. This can be collected in a nonmetal container such as a plastic bottle or wooden cup.

The second method, a **water generator bag**, requires only loose snow but some sort of cloth or material to hold it. If you have the latter, it is quicker to set up than the marshmallow technique. I carry a mosquito head net (with no insect repellent treatment) as a compact, handy bag for this purpose, but a large bandana or a T-shirt will suffice. Fill the cloth, or bag, with uncompacted snow and then suspend it near the fire. Once the fluffy snow at the bottom of the bag becomes saturated, water will drip rapidly.

A head net employed as a water generator bag in northern Sweden.

Collecting Rainwater and Dew

Rainwater can be collected and used directly, with no further treatment. A plastic sheet or tarp is a good means of creating a large surface from which a significant amount of water can be collected. For example, if you have a 10 × 10 ft. (3 × 3 m) tarp and it rains ½ in. (10 mm), the volume of rain incident on the tarp could be as much as 20 gallons (90 liters) (the steeper the angle the tarp is pitched, however, the less water will fall on it). The only caveat is to make sure your tarp is not contaminated with dirt or chemicals such as spray-on waterproofing treatments.

Dew can be collected by soaking a cotton cloth or T-shirt and wringing it out into a container. If local vegetation is long enough (and nontoxic), an efficient way of soaking the materials is to wrap them around your legs and walk through the dew-covered vegetation. They will quickly become soaked. The latter is not a technique I have ever planned to use as a primary means of water collection on a trip, but it is remarkable how much moisture can be mopped up by walking a short distance through wet vegetation.

WATER CONTAMINANTS

In the previous section, we noted we could use rainwater and snow directly, and often springs can be remarkably pure. However, the farther that water travels from these sources, or the longer it sits as surface water, the more likely it is to accumulate contaminants.

To make water safe to drink, you need to eliminate potentially harmful contaminants. The better your understanding of the potential contaminants, the better equipped you will be in determining an appropriate solution.

There are six categories of contaminants you may need to eliminate from fresh water to make it safe to drink:

- turbidity
- chemical pollutants
- parasites (including protozoa)
- bacteria
- viruses
- algal bloom

Turbidity: Turbid water is cloudy. This can be due to suspended hard particulate matter such as mud, sand, silt, and clay, or soft particulate matter such as decomposing organic material from plant and animal debris. Removal of turbidity is important for several reasons: Turbidity can harbor pathogenic organisms. Turbidity can reduce the effectiveness of chemical water sterilization treatments. The particulates in turbid water can irritate your digestive system.

The main flow of turbid, glacial water is being joined by clear nonglacial water. Patagonia, Argentina.

Chemical pollutants can range from herbicides and pesticides to heavy metals. Chemical pollution in recreational outdoor areas and national parks is often associated with nearby mining, forestry, or agriculture. In untouched remote wilderness areas, water is much less likely to be tainted by industrially produced chemicals. When closer to areas of human activity, you should be alert to, and avoid, grossly polluted water with indicators such as dead creatures including fish, invertebrates, or water birds, as well as dead vegetation.

Dead aquatic life can indicate significant pollution.

Parasites are organisms that live in or on another organisms, benefiting at the expense of the other. Waterborne parasites can be either multicellular organisms such as worms and liver flukes, or simple, single-cell organisms such as protozoa.

Some parasites such as liver fluke complete different stages of their life cycle via different hosts, including sheep.

Pathogenic organisms, or simply pathogens, are microorganisms such as protozoa, bacteria, and viruses that cause disease.

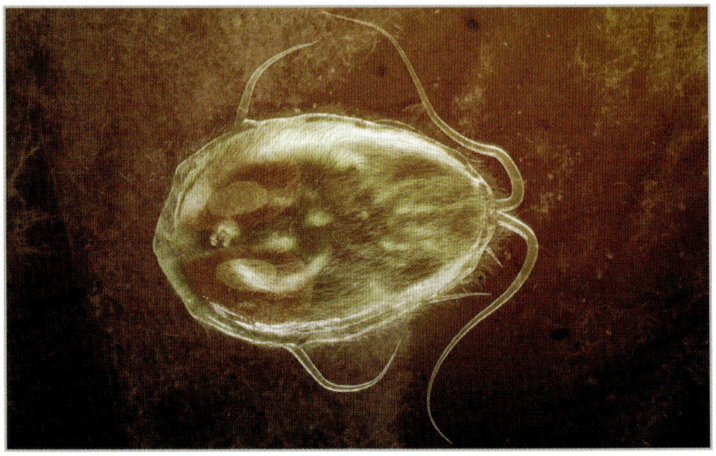

Even the larger pathogenic organisms such as Giardia duodenalis *are microscopic.*

Protozoa are microorganisms that resemble animal cells. They also possess other animallike characteristics such as being capable of motion. They obtain food by ingesting other organisms or organic matter. Many protozoa are free-living microorganisms, but some are parasitic and several cause diseases in humans. Malaria is the most significant protozoan parasite of humans, but this is spread exclusively by mosquito bites. Some pathogenic protozoa can be contracted by drinking contaminated water. These tend to be enteric pathogens that result in gastroenteritis. Protozoa responsible include *Cyclospora cayetanensis*, *Cryptosporidium* spp., *Entamoeba histolytica*, and *Giardia duodenalis.*

Some protozoa have a multistage lifecycle, one stage of which involves the formation of cysts. Cysts allow the organism to live without food, water, or oxygen for a period of time. The cyst protects the organism from harsh conditions, allowing it to be much more resistant to drying, heat, chemicals, crushing, vibration, ultraviolet light, and ionizing radiation than the unprotected organism. This hardiness makes protozoan cysts relatively difficult to kill, compared to bacteria. Protozoa, however, are larger and therefore relatively easy to filter out of water. More on this in the next section.

For parasitic species, the cyst form enables it to survive outside the host and be transmitted to a new host. Transmission of waterborne pathogenic protozoa occurs by the fecal-oral route. After a cyst enters the digestive system of a new host, the organism exits the cyst form and begins to infect the host, replicate, and feed. Further cysts are formed, which are passed into the wider environment with feces, often in the form of diarrhea.

Direct contamination of water sources can be due to poor sanitation. But some protozoa can infect a range of animals, not only humans. Notably this is the case for *Giardia duodenalis* and several *Cryptosporidium* species. Thus, even remote, otherwise-pristine wilderness water sources can contain such pathogenic protozoa.

Bacteria are a large group of single-cell organisms, some of which cause disease. Between them they produce a wide range of infections, some potentially lethal. Bacteria are widely distributed in soil, water, and air, and on—or in—the tissues of plants or animals. So-called traveler's diarrhea is gastroenteritis caused by pathogenic organisms that are often endemic to a local water supply. The bacteria *Escherichia coli* (*E. coli*) is one of the most common bacterial causes of traveler's diarrhea. Other bacterial causes of traveler's diarrhea include species of *Campylobacter, Salmonella,* and *Shigella*. Further examples of diseases caused by waterborne bacteria include cholera, dysentery, leptospirosis, and typhoid fever.

Viruses are not cells. Viruses lack many of the attributes of cells. Only when it is associated with a cell does a virus acquire a key attribute of a living system, reproduction. Many viruses cause disease in the organisms they infect. Infection by waterborne viruses such as *Norovirus* are another significant cause of traveler's diarrhea. Hepatitis A and polio are further examples of viral infections spread through the consumption of water that has been contaminated with human feces.

Algal blooms span several of the categories above. If there is an oversupply of nutrients in relatively warm water, along with increased sunlight, an algal bloom can build up. These occur due to rapid growth of microscopic organisms such as cyanobacteria, formerly known as blue-green algae. This growth can lead to a visible accumulation of algae close to the surface of the water, which looks like scum or blue-green paint. Some types of blooms are toxic and can also secrete toxins into the water. These are potentially harmful to human health.

Freshwater blooms tend to occur in relatively static water. Blooms are less likely to occur in rivers and tend to do so only when they are very slow moving. You should avoid skin contact with algal bloom. If you can source water clear of algal bloom, then it is highly advisable to do so, since backcountry methods of water purification cannot fully remediate the problem.

If you have no choice but to source water where there is algal bloom, then, while you need to remove the visible suspended matter, as you should with other forms of turbidity, you should also understand that there is more than turbidity to deal with. The cyanobacteria should be treated as any other bacteria, plus the potential for toxins in the water means you must treat such water as chemically polluted. Unfortunately, cyanotoxins are not removed from water by most water filters, even those containing activated carbon.

Algal bloom accumulating in a small bay in Cumbria, UK.

A breeze has blown most of the algae to one end of this pond. Algarve, Portugal.

Dealing with Water Contaminants

Water purification requires us to remove particulate matter (turbidity) and chemical pollutants, and to disinfect it from parasites and pathogenic microorganisms. As outdoor people we need techniques that can be applied in the field, using equipment that can realistically be carried into the backcountry. We can't take a municipal water treatment plant with us.

Filtration

Filtration can be separated into coarse filtration and microfiltration.

The aim of **coarse filtration**, or prefiltration as it is sometimes called, is to remove turbidity. This can be achieved with a canvas filter bag, or the intake filter on a microfiltration device, which is typically some sort of metal gauze. Filter bags tend to be most effective but slower. Further, using a filter bag on very turbid water will reduce the chances of clogging a microfiltration device. Coarse filtration does not remove pathogenic organisms. It may, however, reduce the load of pathogens to the extent they are attached to, or contained within, particulate matter being filtered out by coarse filtration. The pathogens themselves are microscopic and can pass through a filter bag.

The aim of **microfiltration** is to filter out at least the larger pathogenic organisms. This includes all protozoa and many bacteria. To achieve this, classic microfiltration devices typically contain fine ceramic filters. The more recent application of hollow-fiber technology and ion exchange technology to backcountry microfilters has resulted in units that will remove most pathogenic organisms, including viruses, which, being the smallest, are hardest to filter out.

Microfilters fall into two broad categories: pump or press filters, which are active, and gravity filters, which are passive. The filters through which water is actively pumped or pressed have the advantage of being faster, whereas gravity filters have the advantage of freeing you to do other tasks while water trickles through the filter.

Some microfilters also contain **activated carbon**, with the aim of removing a wide range of chemical pollutants. Filter units containing activated carbon tend to have a lower total capacity than units without.

A filter bag removing particulate matter from water.

Clear water collecting underneath a filter bag.

A pump-type microfilter.

A gravity microfiltration system. The filter is in the black cylinder.

A press type of microfilter, also containing activated carbon.

A gravity filter in operation.

This type of gravity filter has the microfilter inside the collection bag.

Disinfection

The aim of water disinfection is to kill or deactivate pathogenic organisms. There are three main ways this can be achieved in the field—heat, ultraviolet light, and chemical treatment.

Heat is a highly reliable way to disinfect water. Simply bringing water to a visible rolling boil destroys most organisms. To eliminate *cryptosporidium*, however, the Centers for Disease Control and Prevention (CDC) recommends maintaining a rolling boil for a full minute. This time should be increased to three minutes if you are situated above 6,500 ft. (2,000 m), since water boils at lower temperatures with increased altitude.

Ultraviolet light can be administered in a backcountry setting via the use of a small, portable, battery-powered UV pen designed specifically for water disinfection. The wavelength of ultraviolet light emitted by these devices is effective in neutralizing bacteria, viruses, and protozoa in as little as sixty to ninety seconds, which makes them quicker than boiling and chemical treatments under most circumstances. They are dependent on batteries, however, and can deal with only up to a quart (1 liter) of clear water at a time. It should be noted that water outside the main body of water being treated (such as drops of contaminated water on the threads of a water bottle) will not be disinfected by such a device.

Chemical disinfection treatments need to be effective in neutralizing pathogens but not so toxic that they poison us upon consumption, or over time, if usage is prolonged. Three chemicals are readily available for this purpose—chlorine, iodine, and chlorine dioxide.

Chlorine

Chlorine tablets for water purification are inexpensive and widely available and have no contraindications for extended use. Chlorine has a valuable place as part of your water purification methodologies, but you should understand its limitations. The disinfecting action of chlorine is slow, especially in cold water. It is also quite pH sensitive. If organic residues are present in the water, chlorine binds to them, meaning it is not readily available for disinfection. Chlorine does not kill protozoa. Hence, if chlorine is to be used, a system that filters out organic matter and protozoa should be used first, with chlorine being deployed afterward to destroy remaining bacteria and viruses.

Iodine

Compared to chlorine, iodine is faster, resists inactivation by organic compounds, and is effective over a wider pH range. An iodine concentration of 8 mg/L (eight parts per million) kills bacteria, viruses, and protozoan cysts other than *cryptosporidium*. At this concentration, a contact time of about ninety seconds is required for eradicating bacteria and viruses. For eradicating protozoa, however, a contact time of ten to thirty *minutes* is required; the colder the water, the longer the time. Also, in water of high acidity or alkalinity, iodine is less effective against *giardia*. There are some contraindications for iodine use, including thyroid problems and pregnancy. More generally it is recommended that iodine should not be used for longer than twenty-eight days continuously.

Two widely available forms of iodine applicable to water disinfection are tetraglycine hydroperiodide (TGHP) in tablet form, and tincture of iodine. Iodine tablets deliver 8 mg/L (eight parts per million) when new. A bottle of fifty tablets is small and light and can be carried very easily. The iodine disassociates readily on exposure to air, however, so you should adhere to the stated expiry dates on bottles; else you may underdose.

The standard solution for tincture of iodine for water disinfection is 2 percent iodine and 2.4 percent sodium iodide in 50 percent ethanol. This must be kept in a glass bottle, and it is usually administered with a small glass dropper. Five drops of tincture of iodine 2 percent into a quart of water results in a concentration of 5 mg/L (five parts per million), sufficient to eradicate bacteria and viruses but not protozoa. Being alcohol based, this solution has the advantage that it resists freezing. It's often reported this delivery of iodine results in a stronger taste of iodine than other forms, an assertion I would agree with.

Chlorine Dioxide

As a wilderness water disinfectant, chlorine dioxide is the premium chemical treatment. It eradicates viruses, bacteria, and protozoa, including *giardia* and *cryptosporidium*. While it remains stable in the pH range typically found in natural waters, as well as working adequately in turbid water, it works best in clear water. Unlike chlorine and iodine, chlorine dioxide does not impart a strong flavor. Nor does it have any contraindications. It is, however, relatively expensive, especially compared to chlorine.

Boiling is a straightforward way of eradicating pathogens.

WATER PROCESSING PROTOCOLS

The methods of dealing with water contaminants described above should be combined to create consistently reliable water purification protocols. Your choice of which protocol(s) to employ will depend on the environment, the duration of your trip, the size of your group, weight constraints, mode of transport, availability of fuel, your budget, and, of course, the quantity of water you need to produce each day.

These protocols are not mutually exclusive; you can use more than one on a given trip. For example, one protocol may be more convenient in camp in the evening, while another is more convenient while you are on the move during the day.

Regardless of what you do next, always start with the visibly cleanest source of water you can find. Remember, though, even crystal-clear water can harbor a multitude of pathogenic organisms. Viruses, bacteria, and protozoa are microscopic. You cannot see them with your naked eye.

If the best water you can find is turbid, then you should prefilter it (coarse filtration). This is the first step in any of our protocols, but don't waste your time putting crystal-clear water through a filter bag. The steps that follow in each protocol should be employed in the sequence stated. The order matters.

Protocol A—Step 1: Coarse filtration (if necessary). Step 2: Boil.

This protocol removes turbidity and destroys all pathogenic organisms. It does not remove chemical pollutants. See the remarks in the previous section regarding boiling times. This is a very reliable method for backcountry trips when you are processing unpolluted water and are routinely using a campfire, and there is plenty of fuel. It is not a convenient method for quick stops during the day. If you need to carry fuel for a stove, for example if there is a fire ban or if you are above the treeline, then you should consider the weight of additional fuel for boiling water versus the weight of other purification methods described below.

Protocol B—Step 1: Coarse filtration (if necessary). Step 2: Microfiltration. Step 3: Chlorine disinfection.

This protocol removes turbidity, then removes or destroys all pathogenic organisms. It does not remove chemical pollutants unless the microfilter contains activated carbon (see protocol D). Any microfilter will remove protozoa such as *giardia* and *cryptosporidium*. These are hard to kill with chemical disinfection. Once the water has been through the microfilter, however, you can employ any of the chemical disinfection agents to eradicate remaining bacteria and viruses. Chlorine is the cheapest and most stable. Hence it is in the protocol. But you could also use either iodine or chlorine dioxide. The advantage of this protocol is that it does not require heat. It can also be scaled to your group size, from employing a small microfilter and a personal drinks bottle, to a stirrup-pump-sized microfilter and a jerry can.

A pump-type microfilter in use during a lunch stop on a wilderness canoe trip in Manitoba, Canada.

Protocol C—Step 1: Coarse Filtration (if necessary). Step 2: Chlorine Dioxide Disinfection.

This protocol removes turbidity and eradicates all pathogenic organisms. It does not remove chemical pollutants. This simple protocol has the advantages of not requiring any complex equipment, or requiring fuel and a cooking pot, so it is very lightweight. It's particularly well suited to solo trips and trips of short duration, especially when weight is at a premium. From an economic perspective, however, it doesn't scale well to larger group sizes and longer trip durations, since the cost of the quantity of chlorine dioxide required soon exceeds the cost of a high-quality group microfilter that could serve multiple such trips. A second-rate choice would be to use iodine tablets (TGHP) instead of chlorine dioxide, which would eradicate most pathogenic organisms, except for *cryptosporidium* cysts.

Protocol D—Step 1: Coarse Filtration (if necessary). Step 2: Microfiltration with Activated Carbon. Step 3: Chlorine Disinfection.

This protocol is like protocol B but employs a microfilter device containing activated carbon. This protocol removes turbidity, eradicates all pathogenic organisms, and removes chemical pollutants. This protocol is useful for situations where you suspect the water might be polluted due to agriculture, forestry, or other human activity. Why not use protocol D all the time, rather than protocol B? Because filters with activated carbon in them tend to be more expensive and need replacing more often than microfilters without.

Protocol E—Step 1: Coarse Filtration (if necessary). Step 2: Ultraviolet Light Disinfection.

This protocol removes turbidity and eradicates pathogenic organisms. It does not remove chemical pollutants. This protocol has the advantage of not requiring heat and not introducing chemicals to your drinking water. It is quick to employ but requires the user to employ the UV device correctly and is entirely dependent on batteries.

A microfilter employing ion exchange and activated carbon, a bottle in which water can be sterilized with chlorine dioxide or UV, and a large metal mug that can be used for boiling make for a versatile personal hydration kit.

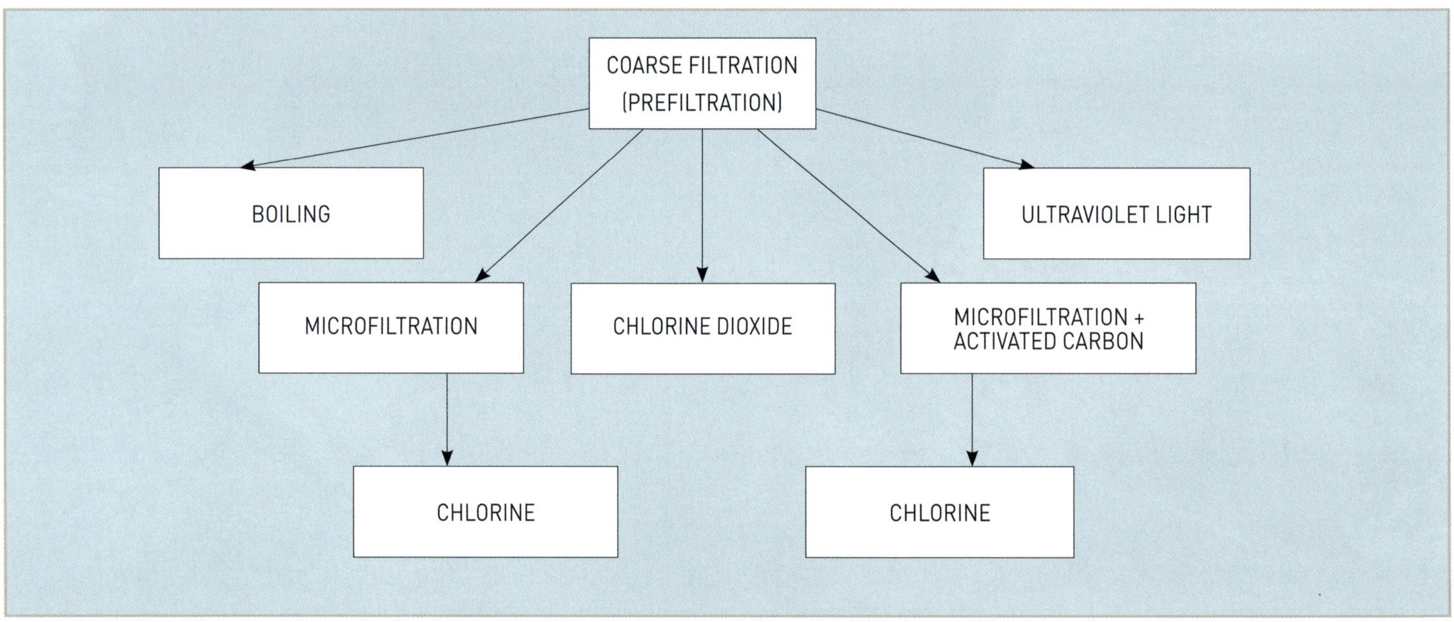

ADDITIONAL WATER CONSIDERATIONS

Disinfecting Threads and Caps

When disinfecting water in a drinks bottle or water bladder, be mindful that untreated water can be on the threads of the container. When using a chemical disinfectant, allow the correct contact time, as per the instructions supplied with the product. Then loosen the cap of the container and flush the threads with treated water from the container. This water contains the active chemical agent and will also disinfect the threads and cap of the container.

Masking Chemical Tastes

Some individuals find the taste of chlorine and iodine objectionable. It is easy to mask or remove the taste of these chemicals from your water by adding ascorbic acid (vitamin C) or a product such as drinks powder or cordial that contains it. Be aware that ascorbic acid not only neutralizes the taste of these chemical disinfectants but also renders them ineffective. So, you must ensure enough time has elapsed and you have flushed the threads before you add any ascorbic acid. Better still, once your water has been disinfected, pour some into a clean cup and flavor it there, not the container in which you undertake the disinfection. This ensures that no traces of ascorbic acid can hinder the next round of disinfection.

Group Water Discipline

In a group setting it is important that straightforward systems are established to prevent people from drinking unprocessed water and to prevent cross-contamination. For example, one system I employ with a group kettle that is used to boil river water is as follows. Once the kettle has been filled it is either put in a known staging area, well away from the fire, or it is placed directly over the fire. Thus, a kettle of unboiled water is never placed next to the fire. Only once the kettle has been brought to a rolling boil is it permitted to be placed *next* to the fire (to keep warm). This way, anyone in the group knows a kettle next to the fire is safe to take water from and there needs to be no communication about whether anyone has seen the kettle boil.

Similarly, if you are using chemical disinfection, store containers that are not yet disinfected separately from those that are ready to be drunk. Make someone responsible for administering the disinfection agent, timing the required contact time, and flushing threads and caps if necessary. Only they move the containers to the "ready to drink" area and everyone else knows to take water only from that area. If there is a group microfiltration device, only those who have been shown how to operate it correctly should be permitted to use it or set it up.

Keep storage containers clean and prevent contamination by implementing procedures to avoid contact with dirty hands (for example, after people have been to the latrine or have been handling raw meat or fish). This could be the use of a hand washing bowl or asking someone else in the group to pour water for you. Replace tops of water containers immediately after use to minimize the risk of dirt, flies, and other contaminants. Avoid cross-contamination by not bringing personal drinking bottles into direct contact with group water storage containers.

Maintaining water safety discipline in a group camping situation requires a system that is explained and understood by everyone. Supervision or oversight may be necessary when children are involved to ensure compliance with the system. Even adults, especially those previously unfamiliar with water purification systems or group hygiene considerations, may need aspects of the system reiterating at first.

Make sure everyone who is involved with water purification is familiar with the system.

Cordage and Bindcraft

Today, we take cordage for granted, with strong synthetic lines readily available and often used in a throwaway fashion. Learning to create your own cordage and bindings from natural materials, however, takes you another step away from total dependence on manufactured goods. Further, having facility with natural binding materials and methods allows you to achieve tasks you couldn't with a hank of nylon line. Plus, if you have modern cordage in your kit, you can reserve its use for where its properties really differentiate it. Another positive consideration for many applications is that natural bindings are biodegradable.

So, in this chapter, we will explore the world of cordage and bindcraft, delving into how to use tree bark and plant fibers. We will also look at the importance of roots, particularly from needled species, as a source of strong bindings. We will also look at the technique of preparing and splitting roots for fine binding applications. The art of withy making will be discussed, using the shoots of species such as willow and hazel to create extremely strong yet flexible binding materials. Knot tying is an essential aspect of this area of know-how, and we will cover knots that are widely applicable to a variety of outdoor situations.

CORE KNOTS

Knots are very useful. They allow you to achieve many things effectively and efficiently in different aspects of outdoor life. Having a solid repertoire of the basic knots allows you to choose the appropriate knot for the job. Having a good knowledge of knots allows you to be able to rely on what you tie. The knots described in this section are core knots that will allow you to undertake most everyday outdoor tasks.

Knot Terminology
bight: A U-shaped curve in the rope without crossing itself
loop: A full circle formed by crossing the rope over itself
working end: The active end used to tie the knot
standing part: The inactive section of the rope
turn: A single wrap around an object or rope
hitch: A knot attaching a rope to an object
bend: A knot joining two ropes

Overhand Loop
This creates a fixed loop. You can tie it anywhere in the line, and you don't need access to the ends of the line.
To tie: Create a bight. Now treat the bight as a single line and tie an overhand knot with the doubled line.

Overhand Knot
The overhand knot, also known as a thumb knot, is the simplest of all knots. It seems to be the most natural and intuitive of all knots. It crops up in many cultures with varied uses and forms the basis of many other knots too. In its basic form, tied in the end of a line, the overhand knot acts as a stopper knot or to stop the end of a line from fraying.
To tie: Make a loop in the rope. Pass the working end through the loop. Pull both ends to tighten.

Fisherman's Knot
Used for joining ropes of equal diameter or forming loops for lanyards or prusiks.
Single fisherman's knot: Lay two rope ends opposing each other with the ropes parallel. Wrap one end around the other rope, creating a loop. Pass the end through the loop and pull tight to form an overhand knot around the other rope. Repeat with the other end, forming a matching overhand knot on the opposite rope. Pull the ropes so that the knots slide together and bind down against each other.
Double fisherman's knot: Add a second wrap to create double overhand knots (double thumb knots) before tightening.

Slipknot

A quick-release overhand knot forming a sliding loop.

To tie: Form a bight in the end of the rope, then take the live end and tie an overhand knot around the standing part. Add an overhand in the end of the rope to stop the loop from pulling open. Alternatively, take the standing part and tie an overhand around the live end to create a noose that will tighten when tensioned, which is useful for snares or binding. Again, add a stopper to the end of the line to increase security.

Jam Knot

The jam knot is a strong binding knot ideal for modern cordage such as paracord. It's particularly effective for creating tight lashings with minimal material, such as when constructing a Roycraft pack frame or ski shoes.

To tie:

1. **Create a stopper knot:** Tie an overhand knot in the working end of the cord and pull it tight.
2. **Wrap the object:** Take the working end around the object(s) you're tying and bring it back toward the standing part.
3. **Form a sliding knot:** Tie an overhand knot around the standing part, creating what is effectively an arbor knot.
4. **Tighten:** Slide the knot snugly against the object but do not overtighten yet.
5. **Invert the slipknot:** Rotate the knot under itself, pulling a bight of the standing part through. Now pull the slipknot down tightly onto the object, maintaining the bight.
6. **Lock off:** Cut the standing part close to the knot and take the standing end through the bight to create yet another overhand knot, pulling it tight to lock everything off. With the remaining end, a final overhand knot can be tied to further lock off the knot.

Figure Eight

This knot is easier to untie than an overhand.

To tie: Make a loop, pass the working end over the standing part, then under and up through the loop. Tighten to form the figure-eight shape. Tie with a bight to create a fixed loop.

Bowline

Creates a secure, easily untied fixed loop.

To tie: Make a loop (the rabbit hole). Pass the working end (rabbit) up through the loop, around the back of the standing part (tree), and down through the loop. Tighten. Secure further with an overhand knot around the loop's line.

Constrictor Hitch

A secure binding knot, like a clove hitch but with an extra tuck. The extra tuck creates a tighter grip than a clove hitch, making the constrictor hitch excellent for binding objects firmly, since it resists slipping and is hard to untie once tightened. A constrictor hitch also copes with the standing part pulling off to the side, not in line with the knot, better than a clove hitch.

To tie: Wrap the working end around the anchor and cross over the standing part. Wrap around the anchor again, then tuck the working end under both the standing part and the first wrap. Pull both the working end and standing part in opposite directions to tighten.

Clove Hitch

A versatile hitch for poles, rings, or bindings.

- **Method 1 (with a bight):** Form two loops. Pass the second loop behind the first and place both over the anchor. Tighten.
- **Method 2 (with the working end):** Wrap the working end around the anchor. Cross it over the standing part, wrap it again, and pass under the standing part. Tighten.

Round Turn and Two Half Hitches

A reliable, versatile knot for securing to a post or tree.

To tie: Wrap the rope around the anchor twice (a round turn). Make a half hitch by passing the working end around the standing part and through the gap created. Make a second half hitch the same way, below the first. Tighten.

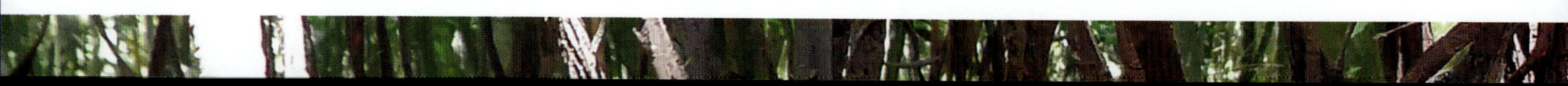

Timber Hitch

A simple, secure hitch for hauling or attaching ropes to trees.

To tie: Pass the working end around the anchor, then back around the standing part. Wrap the working end around itself at least three times and tighten.

Cow Hitch

Also known as the lark's foot or girth hitch, this is useful for attaching loops of ropes, or slings, to objects.

To tie: Pass the loop, or a bight, around the anchor and pull the two loose ends through the bight to tighten.

Sheet Bend

Ideal for joining ropes, especially of unequal thickness.

- **Single sheet bend:** Make a bight in the thicker rope. Pass the thinner rope through the bight, around the back, and under itself. Tighten.
- **Double sheet bend:** Add a second wrap around the bight for extra security before tightening.

Prusik

A friction hitch that grips under tension but slides when slack.

To tie: Wrap a loop of thinner cord around a thicker rope, creating a cow hitch. Wrap each end around the rope again, inside the bight. Tighten and dress the wraps neatly.

A comprehensive set of videos demonstrating how to tie these knots can be found at **https://www.onlinebushcraftcourses.com/knot-knowledge-get-started.**

BINDINGS WITH BARK

In the next section we'll look at processing bark into cordage, but unprocessed bark strips provide quick, easy, and robust binding for many applications, especially campcraft. These strips are flexible, strong, and readily available in many natural environments.

To harvest bark strips, select suitable tree species with flexible and strong bark. In the region in which I live, this is one of the willows, *Salix* spp., or sweet chestnut, *Castanea sativa*. Generally, trees and woody shrubs that possess inner bark suited to cordage making also yield strong strips of bark for bindings.

Harvesting should be done during the growing season, when sap flows, making it easier to remove bark. Don't take bark from a tree's main trunk. Cleanly cut off a side branch or a shoot from a coppice. Also, before cutting additional live material, consider if you have what you need from other materials you have already harvested. For example, green sticks already collected to create a pot-hanging rig may hold enough bark for the fastenings you need.

To remove bark strips from harvested green wood, carefully score the bark, using a sharp knife. Your scoring should be straight and parallel to the long axis of the stick. The knife tip must be inserted sufficiently to cut through the bark to the wood underneath. Once you have two parallel scores, cut across between them to create a long, rectilinear strip. Use your knife tip to raise an edge, or end, of the bark strip so that you can lift it with your fingers. This bark strip can then be pulled away from the wood.

Once you've harvested the bark strips needed, you can use them immediately or let them dry for later use. If you're using them right away, simply trim any excess material and remove any rough edges to create a smooth and flexible strip. For later use, dry the strips in a cool, dark place. They will likely become stiff, but you should be able to rehydrate the strips by soaking them in water until they regain their flexibility.

Unprocessed bark strips can be used for various bindings around camp, such as securing shelters, fastening pot hangers, tripods, or broilers.

A strip of bark has been used to bind the top of a cooking rig.

Bark strips are conducive to several knots that also work well with tape. One such knot is the clove hitch, which is easy to tie and works well with tape-like bark strips. Constrictor hitches are also possible if the bark strip is not too broad.

BINDINGS WITH ROOTS

Tree roots are strong and versatile. Used raw, they make sturdy bindings, but when processed, they can create refined material suitable for tasks such as weaving bags.

A raw root used for a strong binding on part of a shelter structure.

Roots from trees in the pine family—spruce, fir, larch, tamarack, hemlock, and pine—are typically shallow, with thin roots near the surface that are easy to harvest. Birch roots can also work well.

Roots grow straighter in consistent, obstacle-free soil. Search for thin roots radiating from the base of medium-sized trees. Scrape the ground in an arc around the tree to locate roots of the desired diameter.

Long roots of an even diameter make useful binding materials.

If the roots are too thick, move farther from the tree and try again. Once you find a root, expose it by scraping the ground along its length. Use a digging stick to minimize environmental impact. Cut the root to the desired length with a knife, coil it for storage, or use it immediately for tasks such as shelter lashings. Knots such as clove hitch or constrictor hitch are well suited for these bindings.

For refined material, remove the root's outer bark. Use your knife's back to scrape it, or make a simple tool called a brake.

To make a brake: Cut a ⅔in. thick (1.5 cm), 4–6 in. long (10–15 cm) stick. Chamfer one end into a blunt wedge and split it partially along the short axis. Remove some material from the inside of the split to grip the bark. Pull the root through the split to strip the bark efficiently. Alternatively, loosen the bark by wrapping the root around a rough-barked tree and pulling it back and forth to abrade the surface.

Frontier Bushcraft course participants removing the outer bark of roots they have collected.

Once debarked, roots can be used whole or split for a flatter binding surface. Larger roots can be quartered for multiple uses.

To split a root: Start a shallow split at the end, using your thumbnail or knife. Use your fingers to guide the split. If the split veers off to one side, apply more pressure to the thicker side to encourage the split back to the middle. Continue along the root, maintaining an even split.

Split roots can be used immediately or coiled for later use. If they dry out and lose flexibility, soak them in water to restore pliability.

Finger and thumb position for splitting a root with a lot of fine control.

Split spruce roots being used to sew together a bark container.

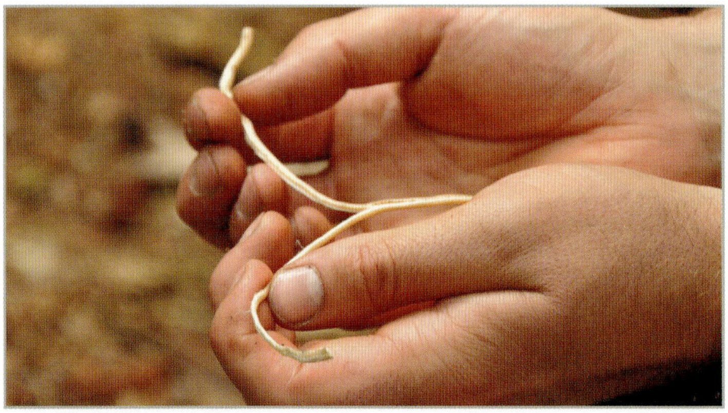

Some people prefer to work this way, though. (Duane Yates)

Bark container sewn with split spruce root.

Split spruce roots, ready for use.

Split spruce root used to bind the barb onto a traditional northwest Pacific coast salmon-trolling hook.

WITHIES

Making withies is an ancient skill for creating strong, flexible bindings from pliable saplings or shoots. Willow and hazel are ideal materials due to their long, evenly thick stems, which withstand twisting. Willows, in particular, are prolific, producing many vigorous side shoots suitable for withies.

Straight shoots on willows create great withies.

Withies are quick to make and incredibly strong, enabling tasks otherwise impossible. Traditional uses include basket making, raft bindings, ski bindings, and bundling firewood. In camp, they serve as bindings for shelter construction, pot-hanging rigs, sawhorses, tables, and wash racks. Twisted withies can also form closed loops by passing their ends through natural kinks, mimicking a timber hitch.

Withies used for traditional ski bindings in Norway.

Other species, such as birch or chestnut, can also be used, though they twist less consistently. In northern forests, green spruce branches are useful substitutes where hazel is unavailable.

A withy used to bind and carry a bundle of firewood.

The author twisting up a hazel withy.

Making a Withy

The key to creating a strong withy is enhancing flexibility while retaining longitudinal strength. Twisting the stem breaks down its structure slightly, allowing fibers to move more freely without losing integrity.

1. **Select a stem**
   - Choose a straight stem, ½–¾ in. (1–2 cm) in diameter, with minimal side branches. Avoid knots, since they hinder even twisting.
   - Retain small side branches at the top—they can aid twisting.

2. **Prepare the stem**
   - Remove small side branches but leave any near the top with a few inches of length.
   - Either leave the stem attached to the tree or cut it and secure the base underfoot for stability.

3. **Start twisting**
   - Twist the stem until you hear a pop or crack, signaling the fibers have loosened.
   - Work above and below the popped section to soften it evenly before moving along the stem.

4. **Use a crank for efficiency**
   - Create a crank in the material being worked (similar in shape to a bicycle crank) to gain mechanical advantage.
   - With the crank in your dominant hand, twist the stem, applying even torque. Guide the twist downward with your nondominant hand.

5. **Maintain consistency**
   - Avoid overtwisting a single area, since it weakens the stem. Conversely, don't move too quickly, leaving untwisted, rigid sections. Aim for smooth, uniform twisting along the entire length.

Withies made from natural materials are an old skill that's rare but valuable to have in the woods. Knowing how to make withies is a valuable addition to an arsenal of cordage and binding materials.

Withies are twisted to increase flexibility but retain the majority of the wood fiber strength.

MAKING CORDAGE FROM NATURAL FIBERS

Natural fibers from plants and trees have been used for cordage since prehistory. Applications include fishing lines, nets, snares, traps, bow drills, and gathering bags. The two-ply twisting method is a core technique for creating strong, versatile cordage.

Sourcing Fibers

Cordage fibers can come from bark, leaves, stems, roots, or other plant parts. Some fibers overlap with those used for fire making but require different preparation. Living green bark is often ideal for cordage, while dry, rotting bark may be better for fire.

Bark: Outer bark fibers are obvious, inner bark fibers less so. Some inner bark fibers can require lengthy processing (see comments on retting further on in this section). Species with bark fibers good for cordage include willows (*Salix* spp.), basswoods and lindens (*Tilia* spp.), cedars (*Thuja* spp.), poplars (*Populus* spp.), junipers, (*Juniperus* spp.), chestnuts (*Castanea* spp.), and *Eucalyptus* species with fibrous barks known as stringybarks.

Leaves: Some leaves can be used directly, or with minimal processing. These are typically long, strap-like leaves that can be twisted up into cordage straight from the plant. Examples include cattail (*Typha* spp.), pendulous sedge (*Carex pendula*), spiny-head mat-rush (*Lomandra longifolia*), and some tree palms (*Livistona* spp.). In addition, some grasses can be twisted up directly into strong cordage. Some leaves need pounding, scraping, or both to release fibers. These tend to be fleshy leaves. Examples include yuccas (*Yucca* spp.), mother-in-law's tongue (*Sansevieria* spp.), sisal, and other agaves (*Agave* spp.)

Stems: Plants such as stinging nettle (*Urtica dioica*), dogbane (*Apocynum cannabinum*), brambles (*Rubus fruticosus* agg.), and fireweed (*Chamaenerion angustifolium*) provide strong stem fibers.

Other sources: Other parts of some plants can also yield cordage-worthy fibers. Examples include coconut husks and cattail rhizomes.

CREATING CORDAGE

1. **Prepare the fibers**

Ensure fibers are clean, dry (unless green), and free from debris.

2. **Start twisting**

Hold a small bundle of fibers. Twist one end away from you until it kinks.

3. **Form a loop**

Bring the kinked portion back on itself to form a loop. Pinch the loop with one hand and keep the strands separated.

4. **Twist and turn**

Twist the far strand away from you, then cross it over the near strand by turning your hand toward you. Repeat, maintaining tension and an even twist.

5. **Splice new fibers**

Overlap new fibers with the existing bundle as needed, incorporating them into the twist.

6. **Finish**

Tie an overhand knot at the end to secure the cordage. Trim excess fibers for a clean finish.

Two-ply cordage twisted up from inner bark fibers.

Nettle Fibers

Stinging nettles provide abundant, reliable fibers. Harvest tall stems by snapping them near the base, wearing gloves if preferred. Strip leaves by running your hand along the stem.

1. **Soften the stems**
   - Place a stem over a hard surface, such as a tree stump or log.
   - Gently tap the stem with a baton or similar tool, focusing on the leaf nodes. This softens the stem and breaks down its structure without damaging the fibers.

2. **Split the stem**
   - Create a lengthwise split starting at the base of the stem, extending it along the entire length. Use your thumbnail for this step.
   - If sections near the leaf nodes are too woody to split, tap them again with the baton to soften further.

3. **Flatten the stem**
   - Once split, open the stem and flatten it into a ribbonlike length.

4. **Identify materials**
   - Observe the two distinct parts:
   - the lighter-colored woody pith (inside)
   - the darker-green outer fibers (outside)

5. **Separate the pith and fibers**
   - Break the brittle woody pith and pull it away from the outer fibers.
   - Discard the pith, keeping the green outer fibers for cordage making.

Inner Bark Fibers

Inner bark fibers from specific tree species can be an excellent source for making cordage. We have two main methods of collection and preparation, depending on the species. Either we'll be collecting inner bark from dead branches or trees, where the bark is rotting to the extent that the inner bark fibers are easily separable by hand, or we'll be cutting green wood, scraping off the outer bark, then removing the fresh inner bark.

Cordage from *Salix* Bark

Salix species, commonly known as willows, have bark containing fibers well suited to cordage. We don't want the outer bark, only the inner bark. Here we collect fresh living wood and remove the inner bark. Cut small-to-medium-sized stems with smooth bark. Older, larger pieces will likely have rough or fissured outer bark, which is harder to scrape away from the inner bark. Ideally, willow bark should be harvested in spring and early summer, when the bark is wettest and most easily separated from the wood.

The process starts with scraping off the outer bark, leaving the inner bark attached to the wood. You can use the back of a belt knife or folding saw (still folded) to scrape off the outer bark. Then score it lengthways before raising an edge with the tip of your knife. If the bark is wet enough, you can remove it all in one piece. Once it's removed, tear the inner bark into strips of a width that suits the diameter of cordage you want to make.

Nettle fibers processed for cordage.

1. Find some smooth-barked shoots of willow of at least an inch (2.5 cm) thickness.

2. *Cut a shoot, then scrape off the outer bark.*

3. *Cut around the fibers of the inner bark.*

4. *Score a straight cut down the shoot.*

5. *Lift the bark with the tip of your knife to begin to separate it from the wood underneath.*

6. *Peel the inner bark away from the wood.*

7. *The inner bark can be pulled into strips as required.*

8. The bark can be used as is, or processed further.

Twisting up processed willow bark. Note the dark-burgundy color.

For basic cordage, let the inner bark strips dry, then rewe and twist them into cordage. The drying will shrink the fibers before you create the cordage, resulting in the cordage retaining a tight twist. This method results in strong cord, but it can become stiff and relatively inflexible after fully drying.

For a more pliable and resilient cordage, you can first process the fibers by boiling them in an alkali solution. The treatment of natural fibers with alkali, known as alkalization, improves resilience, flexibility, durability, and water resistance. Create an alkali solution by mixing campfire wood ash with water. This solution should be heated in a pot over the fire. Soak the bark strips in the hot alkali solution for at least twenty minutes. Then remove them, hang them up, and let them air-dry. After drying, proceed with making cordage as usual.

Strips of willow bark drying after having been heated in a wood ash alkali solution.

Cordage from *Tilia* Bark

There are a group of trees, in the genus *Tilia*, known variously as basswoods, limes, or lindens. Collectively they have a wide distribution across temperate Europe, Asia, and North America. Their inner bark has long, fine fibers, which makes excellent durable cordage. It is ideal for making long lines and fishing nets. When looking to use the bark of *Tilia* species, you have two options. One option is to take fresh bark from cut trees and subject it to a lengthy but highly effective process called retting. The other option is to look for already rotting bark on dead branches or trees that can be used immediately.

Retting

This is a traditional process used to separate fibers from tree bark and the woody stems of plants. The process involves facilitating the action of moisture and microorganisms to break down the pectin and other substances that hold the fibers together within the plant stem or bark. As a result of this decomposition, fibers can be separated more easily. The type of retting employed on fresh *Tilia* bark is water retting. In this method, the material is submerged in water (either stagnant or running) for several weeks. It has been reported that this process can take up to two months in cold water. The bark should be held in place with rocks or sticks, such that it won't float to the surface or move from where you have positioned it.

When retting bark from *Tilia*, you should note that the thickness of the bark will affect the time needed for the retting process. But you should also note that overretting can weaken the fibers. It is therefore important to monitor the progress of the process on a regular basis. As the bark decays, it is normal for it to be become slimy and develop a strong odor.

When the bark reaches a state where it can be separated into fine layers, remove it from the water. You can wash off as much slime as possible at the water's edge. Now separate the fibers and hang them to dry. Once dried, the fibers can be used to make cordage. The length of the basswood fibers means that you will not need to introduce new fibers as frequently when creating cordage, making the process more efficient and the cordage less likely to contain areas of weakness.

Immediate Use

For bark fibers that can be used immediately, look for older branches or dead trees with rotting bark. The fibers should be easily pulled out of this bark, and they can be used directly for cordage making. The fibers will not necessarily come away in lengths as extensive as fresh bark fibers, since some sections may be so rotten that the fibers are no longer viable for cordage making. Weak or short sections of fibers from rotten bark that you reject for cordage making can be dried and used as tinder bundles for fire lighting.

The fibrous outer bark of western red cedar, Thuja plicata.

Useful Trees and Plants

Knowing which trees and plants are useful, and what to do with them, is one of the cornerstones of bushcraft. The materials, foods, and medicines they provide are all around us, but they become available only once you can recognize them and understand their properties. A good working knowledge of trees and plants means you can gather firewood with confidence, find cordage fibers, collect edible greens, or identify species with medicinal qualities. Moreover, this knowledge helps you avoid mistakes, since many look-alikes exist, and some of them are unpleasant or even dangerous.

This chapter focuses on species that are widely distributed, easily identifiable, and directly useful to the bushcrafter. The trees and plants covered here provide a practical core. They represent numerous resources that we can utilize immediately. They also give you a strong base upon which you can further grow your knowledge. Learn these well and you'll quickly find the same or closely related species farther afield, with similar uses. In doing so, you'll begin to build a skill that connects across environments. You'll have the ability to identify what is most readily available and valuable in the landscape, plus put it to work.

In terms of uses, I have included species or genera that are most useful for the beginner, the itinerant bushcrafter, or the individual who has found themselves in a survival situation, rather than from the perspective of an indigenous economy. The species highlighted here provide resources that you can access as soon as you arrive in an environment.

Where tree or plant names are different in the USA (or Canada) from the UK and other English-speaking nations, I have supplied the relevant local common name (e.g., basswood). But there are also multiple common names for some species, even within the UK, never mind the USA; hence the importance of scientific names. Scientific names represent the one correct name for each species.

ESSENTIAL TREES

What follows is an overview of arguably the most important trees for bushcraft and survival in the northern temperate and boreal forests.

Broad-Leaved Trees

The Alders

Alders form the genus *Alnus*. They are deciduous and mainly occur in the northern temperate zone. Alders like being close to water, growing near streams and pools and in wet ground. As such, alders act as water indicators. Seen from a distance, they can indicate the presence of a watercourse. Dead, standing alder of small to medium diameter is a good source of the friction parts of bow-drill sets and is a reliable material for this method of ignition. Alder wood has traditionally been used for smoking fish on both sides of the Atlantic.

The Ashes

Ashes form the genus *Fraxinus*. They are widespread deciduous trees, found in Eurasia and North America. Ash wood is typically tough yet springy, which makes it resilient. These qualities have made it a choice wood for bows and axe handles as well as other uses that require its properties. Ash is also very good firewood. Due to low moisture content it will burn green but, such as other woods, is still better firewood when seasoned.

Alders like to grow near water and in wet areas.

Many ash species, such as this European common ash, have pinnately compound leaves.

The Beeches

Beeches form the genus *Fagus*, which has members through Eurasia and from Canada to Mexico. Beeches are deciduous, but you may see dead leaves remaining on immature specimens through the winter as well as on the lower branches of larger trees. The buds tend to be spindle shaped, with points. The edible nuts have a four-part casing that opens to reveal two three-sided nuts inside. You can snack on them raw, but you get more nutritional value from them cooked. Beech trees are dangerous to camp under since they tend to drop large limbs, particularly in springtime. Dropped limbs provide a very good source of firewood, though. Beech burns hot and embers are very good for roasting food. In the spring, brand-new, light-green beech leaves are edible for a little while after they emerge from the buds. They are surprisingly tasty.

European common beech leaves.

The Birches

Birches form the genus *Betula*. These fast-growing, relatively short-lived deciduous trees are the woodsman's friend. They have many uses. For starters, the bark is a renowned natural fire lighter, probably the best in the Northern Hemisphere. The bark lights easily from a small flame or a spark, and the oils it contains mean it burns strongly and for a good amount of time, allowing kindling to be easily ignited from it. Birches also provide good kindling, in the form of matchstick-thin sticks. Green birch wood is relatively easy to carve and is the source of many hand-carved spoons and cups. Seasoned birch wood burns well. Birch roots can be used for bindings, sap can be tapped in the spring, and the leaves contain saponins—a natural soap. Birches are easy to recognize, with peeling bark, often silvery or light colored, with horizontal lenticels. Further, the bark from a number of species, removed in sheets, lends itself to making containers. Strips of bark can also be woven into baskets, quivers, or even shoes. Large sheets of bark have been used for covering shelters and, of course, for making birchbark canoes. Dry distillation of the bark yields the oils it contains, which can be put to several uses on its own or combined with other materials; for example, to make a thermoplastic glue. Birch can also be used for friction fire lighting with the bow-drill technique, although it would not be my first choice.

Birches are an incredibly useful pioneer species.

Birch bark holds many valuable uses.

The Hazels

Members of the genus *Corylus* are better known as hazels. This is a small genus, but its members are widely distributed in the Northern Hemisphere. The edible fruits—more commonly referred to as hazelnuts or cobnuts—are the common feature that binds this genus. As well as the food value of the nuts, hazels provide a good source of materials for many items around camp, particularly those that require relatively thin but stiff poles, such as pot hangers, wauguns, cranes, and the like, as well as poles and pegs for tarp setups. Hazel staffs also make good walking sticks and thumb sticks. Twisted up into a withy, hazel provides the source of one of bushcraft's strongest bindings.

The Limes and Basswoods

Known as lime or linden in Europe, and basswood in North America, these species form the genus *Tilia*. They are deciduous trees found all around the Northern Hemisphere. The English name "lime" has a common root with the word "line," as in cordage. This gives some indication of the historical importance of these species for making cordage and ropes, particularly in the times prior to fibers such as jute being available from farther afield. To this day, *Tilia* species remain one of the top sources of fibers for cordage in the woods. In turn, this allows the manufacture of traps, fishing nets, and other applications that require good-quality, strong cordage. The fibrous inner bark also lends itself very well to making bird's nest type of tinder bundles. The wood of limes and basswoods is light and carves very nicely, making good spoons, ladles, and scoops. The grain is fine, with the action of carving the wood feeling buttery smooth. This smoothness is also experienced when using the wood for the friction parts of bow-drill sets. Lime or basswood bow drills are not only silky smooth in operation but also very effective, being one of the better woods you can choose for the purpose. Like beech leaves, the leaves of basswood can be eaten when very young in the spring.

Edible nut from the North American beaked hazel, Corylus colurna.

Basswood leaves are rounded, heart-shaped leaves with asymmetrical lobes.

The Maples

Compared to other genera here, the maples, *Acer*, form quite a large genus. They are largely deciduous trees found around the Northern Hemisphere from western North America to eastern Asia. The wood is durable yet light and carves nicely. Thus it makes good spoons and cooking utensils. The wood is also good for friction fire lighting. Indeed, my first bow-drill fire was lit with wood from a maple.

The Oaks

Oaks belong to the genus *Quercus*. They have distinctive lobed leaves. Some species are magnificent, long-lived deciduous trees, revered for their strength. These trees have dense and heavy wood. As such, it is difficult to carve, but items made from oak wood tend to be very resilient. Oak provides some of the finest firewood, burning slow and steady, producing excellent embers for roasting and cooking in a camp oven. Some North American species are less dense than European species but still make good firewood. Oak bark holds significance in traditional tanning processes due to its high tannin content. The inner bark, which is fibrous, can be separated when rotting away from the wood. When dried, this can be used as a fine kindling. With a few exceptions, the acorns produced by oaks are typically high in tannins, so they cannot be consumed directly from the tree. But they are potentially very nourishing. Before they can be used for food, the tannins need to be leached from the acorns. Despite this, acorns have historically provided significant sustenance across the Northern Hemisphere, sometimes as a staple food. They were often ground into flour, made into bread and pancakes, added to soups and stews, or, with added moisture, eaten as tasty, nutritious mush, such as porridge.

Maple leaves typically have an easily identifed five-lobed shape.

Oaks have distinctive lobed leaves.

Willows and Poplars

Willows, *Salix*, and poplars, *Populus*, are closely related—both in the family Salicaceae. Moreover, they share many features, both in terms of identification but also uses. Willows send up vigorous shoots, which are good for basket weaving, fish traps, and the like. They can also be twisted up into excellent withies. The bark of these species contains natural compounds that are related to aspirin. The wood splits well, is fine grained, and makes both good feathersticks and bow-drill sets. The inner bark of these species is typically fibrous. The whole bark can be used for simple tapes and straps for lashings, or the inner bark can be separated and then processed into more refined cordage. Willows like to grow in damp ground or near water. They are a very good water indicator. The wood of poplars is typically quite light in weight yet relatively durable. It makes lightweight canoe paddles and snow shovels. The inner bark of poplars, when beginning to rot, can make very good fine kindling for taking embers to flame.

A good number of willows and poplars have diamond-shaped markings on their bark.

Evergreen Trees

The Cedars

Also known as the arbor vitae, cedars are in the genus *Thuja*. This is a small genus of trees with members in Asia and North America. The North American species—eastern white cedar (*Thuja occidentalis*) and western red cedar (*Thuja plicata*)—are incredibly important species for traditional lifeways. These species have also been planted more widely for forestry and ornament. Cedars have fibrous bark, which lends itself to cordage, ropes, baskets, and matting, even having been woven finely enough to make blankets, as well as the fibers being used as tinder bundles. The wood is fine grained and splits very well. On a day-to-day practical level in the bush, it is a very good source of material for feathersticks. Traditionally, cedar has been used for canoe ribs since it can be split down thin and then steam-bent. Cedar wood carves nicely both for ornament as well as for practical items such as bowls. The wood is highly effective for friction fire lighting, both the spindle and hearth of bow-drill sets as well as the hearth board of hand-drill sets. The roots can be utilized as bindings. Arbor vitae literally means tree of life. These species have many medicinal properties and were used as such by First Nations. In particular, cedars have a good amount of vitamin C in their leaves. This can be used to prevent or treat scurvy, and there are some celebrated cases of natives helping European sailors in this manner.

Cedars are also known as arbor vitae, literally "tree of life."

The Pines

Pinus is a genus within the family Pinaceae. These are the pines, a genus of evergreen needled trees, common and widespread around the Northern Hemisphere. Except for single-leaf piñon pines, all pines have their needles held in at least pairs. This helps differentiate pines from other needled species, including toxic yews, *Taxus* spp. The pines have many uses. Their resinous wood burns fast and with a good amount of light. Relatively knot-free sections of straight-grained species lend themselves well to feathersticks and splints of kindling, for which turpentine-rich lengths are particularly good. If the wood is bone dry and not too resinous, it makes for a successful bow-drill set too. Pine roots can be used for bindings. The needles are rich in vitamin C and make a pleasant hot beverage. The seeds or pine nuts of some species are large enough to harvest and are highly nutritious. Inner bark of some pines have been harvested for food in both Eurasia and North America.

Pine needles emanate at least in pairs and make for a flavorsome vitamin C–rich hot beverage.

The Spruces

The spruces are evergreen needle-leafed trees in the genus *Picea*. The spruces may have a narrower range of uses, but they are one of the most prolific genera of trees on the planet, forming much of the northern forests of Eurasia and North America. The needles can range from being quite sharp, stiff, and spiky to relatively pliable and blunt. The latter foliage forms good flooring and bedding materials, particularly important as insulation from the ground or snow in more-northerly climes. The density of foliage on spruce boughs also makes them a very good thatching material for shelters. The lower reaches of these trees also typically yield many dead small twigs and sticks, protected from rain and snow by the dense foliage above, forming a ready store of kindling. This resinous wood burns well, and these small sticks are often my first port of call for fire lighting in the northern forests. Spruce resin is highly flammable and useful in lighting fires, particularly in damp conditions when no birch bark is available. The needles can be employed to make a tea. The roots of spruces form excellent, strong bindings, both raw from the ground for shelters, cooking tripods, and other structures, as well as debarked and split for more-refined bindings.

Familiar as a Christmas tree to many, the spruces are one of the most prolific genera of trees on the planet.

The trees listed in this section provide a solid foundation that you should be able to put to practical use almost immediately. Moreover, if you already know—or soon learn—species in these genera close to where you live, as you travel farther afield you will find similar, closely related species with similar uses and value from a bushcraft and survival perspective.

ESSENTIAL PLANTS

The following list of plants should be combined with those mentioned elsewhere in this book but, to save space, not repeated here, particularly those mentioned in the chapters on fire and cordage. While this is far from being exhaustive, I believe the plants highlighted in this book provide the basis for a good foundational knowledge, useful for bushcraft in many areas, especially outside the tropics.

The plants mentioned below have widespread distributions. Many have been spread farther afield by human activity, including across oceans. Many plants native to Eurasia are naturalized in North America, Australia, and New Zealand, for example. They might be so well established they are considered an invasive weed. Even so, not all the plants in this section occur in the same area. First get to know those in your area, then expand from there. You will be well on your way to having a solid base of useful plants relevant to you.

All included plants have been selected for their value in general utility, food, and medicine—and have been arranged alphabetically. Furthermore, the uses are all directly applicable, without much processing.

WARNING
Be certain about the positive identification of wild edibles, since nonedible varieties can be highly toxic. Also be wary of eating any aquatic plants uncooked, not because the plant is necessarily an issue if consumed raw, but the water they are in is likely to contain parasites and pathogens.

***Achillea millefolium*, yarrow**, appears to be one of the oldest known plant medicines, being among six medicinal plants whose pollen was found in a Neanderthal grave, dated to 65,000 years ago. It is well known as a herb for staunching wounds, one that Achilles is reputed to have told his soldiers to carry. The leaves, picked green, crushed, then applied to a fresh wound, work to reduce bleeding. Equally, dried leaves, finely crushed, work as a natural hemostatic powder and seem to promote healing in a faster time than without using it. Yarrow also has a reputation for reducing inflammation. Modern scientific studies have shown that extracts of yarrow have antioxidant and antimicrobial properties.

Yarrow. Ontario, Canada.

Allium. This genus contains wild onions, garlic, leeks, and chives, as well as familiar cultivars. With over 1,000 species, this genus is large. *A. ursinum*, **ramsons**, and *A. tricoccum*, **ramps**, are favorites of foragers. Some wild *Allium* species don't form much, if anything, of a bulb so are targeted for their flowers and leaves. Other species form a more developed bulb that can be worth harvesting. Examples include *A. canadense*, *A. textile*, *A. cernuum*, and *A. vineale*. Care must be taken, however, to avoid mistaking other bulb-forming plant species, of which there are several notable poisonous species, some of them potentially deadly. These include, but are not limited to, plants in the following genera: *Hyacinthoides* (bluebells), *Galanthus* (snowdrops), *Narcissus* (daffodils), *Nothoscordum* (*N. bivalve* is known as crow poison or false garlic), and the various plants called death camas, which fall into the genera *Toxicoscordion*, *Anticlea*, *Stenanthium*, and *Zigadenus*. Similarly, for those seeking broad-leaved species such as *A. ursinum*, there are some poisonous look-alikes to avoid, including *Convallaria majalis*, lily of the valley, and the young leaves of *Arum* species. None of these poisonous species smell like onions, however. So, don't eat anything that appears to be an onion but doesn't smell like one.

Ramsons. Cumbria, UK.

Apocynum cannabinum, **dogbane**. Fibers from dead stems make excellent cordage. Note the plant is toxic, containing cardiac glycosides, so don't rewet the fibers in your mouth.

Dogbane. Ohio, USA.

Arctium, the **burdocks**. In Asia, burdock is cultivated as a root vegetable. The roots contain a significant amount of starch, including the indigestible inulin but also digestible carbohydrate. In the wild they favor hard ground, often requiring significant effort to dig up. The roots taste best if cut into small pieces and then fried but can also be added to stews. The plants are biennial, so you should target the roots of plants toward the end of their first year of life, or the beginning of the second. Leaf stems and young leaves are edible but often horribly bitter. Boil, changing the water to improve the taste. Larger leaves make an effective protective wrap for food when cooking under a fire, without imparting bitterness. Avoid mistaking for the poisonous foxglove, *Digitalis*, species.

Arctostaphylos. This genus contains the woody shrubs known as **manzanitas** and the dwarf shrubs known as **bearberries**. Manzanitas, found mainly in the West of North America, form edible berries, and their evergreen leaves have antiseptic qualities. Bearberries, while quite insipid, traditionally have been eaten, usually being mixed with other foods. Probably the best-known bearberry, *A. uva-ursi*, has a circumpolar distribution and, despite the fruits being dry and mealy, was widely used as food. Its leaves were added to traditional smoking mixtures known as **kinnikinnick**, and this plant is sometimes referred to by that name too.

Burdock. Ontario, Canada.

Common bearberry. Manitoba, Canada.

Manzanita. Utah, USA.

Argentina, the **silverweeds**. The roots of silverweeds have provided an important source of starch, and thus calories, either as a famine food or even a staple. While the roots might be small, the plants can be found growing in swards that are easily excavated with a digging stick. The leaves of silverweed are soft and have been used to cushion sore feet from aggravating footwear.

Atriplex, the **saltbushes** and **oraches,** are distributed almost worldwide. The plants retain salt in their foliage, and leaves of edible species taste salty. As a rule, the foliage should be cooked. The seeds of many species can be used for food, being added to stews, cooked into a porridge, or ground for flour. Examples include *A. nummularia*, **old man saltbush**, native to Australia; *A. canescens*, **four-wing saltbush**, native to the USA; and *A. patula*, **common orache**, native to northern Europe. See also the closely related genus *Chenopodium* (page 145).

Silverweed. Sussex, UK.

Oldman saltbush. Victoria, Australia.

Bistorta, the **bistorts,** occur throughout much of the Northern Hemisphere. Many species of bistorts have been, and still can be, used for food. Young leaves are eaten raw; shoots and mature leaves steamed or boiled; starchy roots boiled, fried, or roasted.

Basal leaves of common bistort. South Yorkshire, UK.

Flowering stems of common bistort. Sussex, UK.

Brassicaceae is a family of over 4,000 plants, commonly known as the cabbage family, almost all of which are nontoxic and edible in some way. A notable exception is the genus *Erysimum*, most members of which contain toxic cardiac glycosides. Many folks are familiar with domesticated cultivars such as cabbages, kale, cauliflower, broccoli, brussels sprouts, turnips, radishes, and rapeseeds, including canola. **Rocket**, a.k.a. arugula (*Eruca vesicaria)*, **horseradish** (*Armoracia rusticana*), and **watercress** (*Nasturtium officianale*), as well as a variety of mustards and cresses, are commonly cultivated but can also be found growing wild in their native habitat or naturalized farther afield. A widespread native of Eurasia that has become a problematic invasive species in North America is *Alliaria petiolata*, **garlic mustard**. Its leaves are edible raw or cooked. Seeds can be used for flavoring. But note there is some evidence that young plants can contain a cyanogenic glycoside; this can be eliminated by chopping the leaves and allowing exposure to air.

Watercress. Arizona, USA.

Garlic mustard. County Durham, UK.

***Chamaenerion angustifolium*, fireweed**, a.k.a. rosebay willowherb. Roots can be roasted to provide complex carbohydrates (best before flowering). Tender spring shoots make a nice green vegetable providing vitamin C and provitamin A. Young stems (before they become woody) can be peeled and eaten raw. Leaves are used to make teas, either directly, dried, or fermented. Flowers can be included in teas or added to salads. Pith from mature stems can be consumed raw (usually sweet, sometimes a little spicy), cooked (added to stews/soups is good), or fermented. Stem fibers are used for natural cordage. The downy seed material can be used for fire lighting. Native peoples also used this fluff for insulation, mixed with other materials for weaving into blankets.

Chenopodium, commonly known as **goosefoot**. Like the closely related *Atriplex*, this genus has an almost worldwide distribution. They have a history of use as food dating back thousands of years, including *C. album*, **white goosefoot,** *C. pallidicaule*, **cañihua**, and *C. berlandieri*, **pitseed goosefoot**. The most well-known member of this genus is probably *C. quinoa*, **quinoa**. The term **lamb's quarters** or **lambsquarters** is, confusingly, applied to *C. album* in Europe and *C. berlandieri* in North America. **Fat hen** is often applied to *C. album* but also used to refer to other species. The edible seeds are typically small but nutritious, while the leaves of some species are valued as a green.

Fireweed. County Durham, UK.

Goosefoot. Campania, Italy.

Filipendula ulmaria, **meadowsweet**, is an upright plant of damp ground, beside streams, ditches, ponds, and lakes. It has crinkly, toothed side leaves with a three-lobed terminal leaf, any of which when crushed smell medicinal, reminiscent of a muscle rub mixed with cucumber. This smell-a-like comparison with products such as Ralgex (Deep Heat) is likely no coincidence since the product contains salicylates, as does meadowsweet. Some people also smell a similarity between meadowsweet and Germolene, which was originally formulated with the inclusion of oil of wintergreen. In addition to salicylates, meadowsweet also contains tannins and various glycosides, including gaultherin (which is also found in wintergreen species, *Gaultheria*). The presence of these compounds has long seen meadowsweet used as a medicinal herb, particularly good for cold, flu, indigestion, and other stomach upsets. It's soothing and calming, and the simplest way to use the fresh leaves is to make a tea with them. I find it tastes nice too, which is always a bonus when it comes to medicines.

Meadowsweet. County Durham, UK.

Juncus is a genus of plants commonly known as **rushes**. As a group, they have a wide natural distribution, and where they occur, stem material can be used for making bindings, cordage, bags, pouches, and baskets. Early shoots of some species were eaten in the spring. The dried stem pith can be used as a tinder. The pith of some species, particularly *J. effusus*, was dipped in tallow to create rushlights.

Common rush. Cumbria, UK.

Juniperus is a genus of evergreen shrubs and trees in the cypress family, known as **junipers**, widely distributed around the Northern Hemisphere. Indeed, common juniper, *J. communis*, is the world's most widely distributed woody plant species. The female cones of many juniper species, commonly referred to as berries, are used to flavor food dishes, and some have been used as famine foods. Fibrous outer bark makes decent cordage and has been used for basket making. Dried, shredded bark is a good source of fibers for a bird's-nest tinder bundle for taking an ember to flame. Moreover, dead juniper wood is very good for bow-drill friction fire lighting. The wood is tough, yet manageable to carve, lending itself to a range of applications from rabbit sticks to utensils.

Common juniper. Inverness-shire, UK.

Utah juniper. Arizona, USA.

***Myrica gale*, bog myrtle**, a.k.a. sweet gale. Rubbing fresh leaves onto your skin and into your hair is an effective insect repellent. The catkins can be used as fishing lures. Thin dead twigs make good kindling.

A patch of bog myrtle in the Scottish Highlands.

Bog myrtle. Ontario, Canada.

Plantago is a genus of about 200 species known as **plantains**. Many species have uses in common. For example, **broadleaf plantain**, *P. major*, and **ribwort plantain**, *P. lanceolata*, are widespread Eurasian species that have become widely naturalized across many other regions worldwide. Their edible leaves are best steamed or boiled. Their seeds can be eaten raw, boiled like sago, or ground into flour for baking. Crushed leaves or spit poultices are traditionally used to draw out splinters, dirt, and pus from wounds, as well as to staunch bleeding and promote healing. Strong decoctions of the leaves serve as mouthwashes for gum infections and ulcers, while syrups and teas are valued remedies for persistent coughs and phlegm. Several other plantains are also valued for their mucilage-rich seeds, which can help relieve some digestive complaints, including constipation. Of particular note in this regard are *P. indica*, **branched plantain**, a.k.a. black psyllium, and *P. ovata*, **blond psyllium**. Other notable plantains with edible leaves include *P. coronopus*, **buck's-horn plantain**, a.k.a. minutina or erba stella. *P. asiatica*, **Chinese plantain**, has been used in traditional medicine for similar applications as described for other plantains, as well as the leaves being used in Asian cooking. There are twenty-four species native to Australia, where they are commonly known as **sago weeds** after the use of the mucilaginous seeds to make a kind of porridge. *P. debilis* was used by Aboriginals to treat sprains, ulcers, and boils.

Broadleaf plantain. Ontario, Canada.

Ribwort plantain. Staffordshire, UK.

Prunella vulgaris, **self-heal**, a.k.a. heal-all. I've encountered this plant in Europe, North America, and Australia. Traditionally the main European uses of self-heal were staunching bleeding and healing wounds, relieving colds and fevers, and treating throat and mouth infections and sores. For wounds, a poultice of leaves is applied directly. For colds and fevers, the leaves (and flowers if available) are steeped to make a tea, which can also be used as a mouthwash or gargle for mouth and throat problems. Modern scientific studies have shown *P. vulgaris* to contain antiviral compounds, including Prunellin, as well as possessing antibacterial, antimicrobial, and anti-inflammatory properties.

Self-heal. Sussex, UK.

Pteridium is a widespread genus of ferns commonly called **bracken**, also referred to as eagle ferns. The unfurling young shoots or fiddleheads of some species are harvested in the spring and eaten as a vegetable. As a rule, however, this is not advisable. Some species contain concentrations of carcinogens as well as the antinutrient thiaminase. The roots of the plants can be processed into edible carbohydrate, but this involves a considerable amount of work, involving several stages. So, unlike other underground storage organs that can be unearthed, eaten raw, or cooked directly, bracken rhizomes do not present an immediately consumable source of calories. Bracken tends to grow in large stands. Fully grown plants can be harvested in quantity, bundles of which make a viable shelter covering. Do not attempt to pull plants from the ground with bare hands, though; the edges of stem fibers are extremely sharp and can easily cause nasty lacerations. Instead, stems should be cut. Dead, dry bracken stems and fronds make good kindling, the fronds making highly effective tinder bundles.

Austral bracken. NSW, Australia.

Ribes are **currants** and **gooseberries**. The fruits are edible raw, cooked, or made into a jelly. The tartness of the fresh fruits comes from their acidity. They contain, among other acids, a significant amount of ascorbic acid (vitamin C). For example, redcurrants have a concentration of about 40 mg / 100 g fruit.

Wild gooseberry. Ontario, Canada.

Redcurrant. Sussex, UK.

Rosa is the genus of **roses**, within the wider rose family, Rosaceae. Rosehips, the fruits of roses, are highly nutritious, containing a range of vitamins and minerals. Concentrations of vitamin C found in rosehips are much higher than many familiar fruits, including oranges. Rosehip flesh can be eaten raw. First remove the hairy seeds from the center of the hip. Rosehips can also be made into syrup or even soup. The stems of some rose species have sizable, sturdy thorns that can be used to improvise fishhooks.

Rubus is another genus in the family Rosaceae, containing **blackberries**, **raspberries**, **dewberries**, and **cloudberries**. For good reason the fruits of these plants are some of the more widely known wild edibles. They are easy to recognize and often abundant. Plus they represent some of the most delicious wild fruits to eat straight from the bush. Young leaves can often be used for tea. Fibers from the long stems of brambles, *R. fruticosus* agg., make strong cordage.

Dog rose. County Durham, UK.

Brambles. Sussex, UK.

***Sagittaria latifolia*, arrowhead**, a.k.a. wapato, swamp potato, or duck potato, is an aquatic plant with an arrowhead-shaped leaf. This plant is native to North America and was an important food source to some First Nations. The tuber at the base of the plant is an edible source of starch, resembling a small white or bluish potato.

Arrowhead. USA.

***Sambucus*, the elders**, or elderberries, are a group of shrubs found in North America, South America, Eurasia, and Australasia. The ripe fruits of many species have long been consumed by humans, but the fresh parts of these plants, including most fruits, contain cyanogenic glycosides. These compounds are, however, destroyed by heat. Hence, it is best to cook the fruits. The larger, woody species produce secondary shoots that lend themselves well to the manufacture of hand drills for friction fire lighting. These pith-filled shoots can also be fashioned into straws for sip wells.

European black elder. Roxburghshire, UK.

White elderberry. Victoria, Australia.

Sphagnum is a genus of mosses. **Sphagnum moss** is highly absorbent. It can be used as a wound dressing, sanitary pad, or diaper liner. Further, it has qualities that limit bacterial growth. It can be used as padding for improvised beds and chinking to weatherproof more-permanent shelters.

***Taraxacum* agg., dandelions**, all display similar characteristics with strongly toothed leaves, giving rise to the name "Dent de Lyon," literally "tooth of the lion." Leaves are typically bitter, with the younger leaves sometimes being less so. They can be added to salads with other less bitter leaves or blanched to remove some of the bitterness. The small taproots are a viable source of starch. They can also be dried and roasted in such a way as to produce an ersatz coffee. Stems have been used for cordage. These plants are often considered a weed. Don't overlook them, especially, as a food resource.

Sphagnum moss. Aberdeenshire, UK.

Dandelion. East Sussex, UK.

Typha is a small genus of plants known as **cattails**, **reedmace**, **bulrush**, or **cumbungi**. From a bushcraft and survival perspective, these are wonder plants. There are uses for every part of the plant. The leaves can be woven into matting, coverings, or lightweight containers or twisted up to form cordage. The green flower spikes can be boiled and eaten. The edible yellow pollen can be collected in large quantities. I find it good mixed with regular flour to make a fry bread or pan bread. The seed heads yield abundant fluff that will readily accept a spark for fire lighting. This fluff was traditionally used as insulation in clothing or stuffing in pillows. The upper stems can sometimes provide an acceptable hand drill, although they are often too fragile. The lower part of the stem can be eaten, being something like a flavorless leek, and the pointed, young shoot tips make a pleasant crunchy vegetable. The rhizomes are a rich and abundant source of digestible starch, the most expedient way of rhizome cooking being roasted directly on hot embers. There are other more involved methods of removing the starch, which are worthwhile if you want to make some flour for storage and later use. Once the starch has been removed, the fibers from the rhizomes make good cordage, far better than the leaves do. These plants have multiple traditional medicinal uses, including the gelatinous substance from between the leaf bases being used as a topical salve.

Cumbungi. Victoria, Australia.

Greater reedmace. East Sussex, UK.

Cattails. Ontario, Canada.

***Urtica dioica*, stinging nettle**. This plant, and its hypodermic, histamine-injecting hairs, is likely familiar to many. The stems are a source of excellent cordage fiber. Nettles provide one of the more substantial leafy wild foods. Nettle leaves are highly nutritious, containing a surprising amount of protein for a green plant. Nettles taste pretty good, too, and retain an agreeable texture when cooked. Leaves can be wilted by passing a whole stem over an open fire. The top-most leaves are the most tender, great when blanched to create a spinach-like green, or added to soups. For a simple herbal tea in the field, the leaves, steeped in hot water, make a pleasant beverage. Not only is nettle tea pleasant, it also has a good number of recorded health benefits as well as having been used medicinally on both sides of the Atlantic.

Vaccinium. This genus contains a variety of edible berry forming plants, including **cranberries**, *V.* subg. *Oxycoccus*. The raw fruit of **cowberry**, or lingon, *V. vitis-idaea*, is quite unpalatable. The unpleasant taste comes from the presence of benzoic acid and oxalic acid, both of which should be consumed only in moderate quantities. The berries make a pleasant fruit leather, though. Also, with the addition of some pectin from apples, a good jelly can be made. The high quantity of benzoic acid acts as a natural preservative making fresh cowberries easy to store. By contrast, **blueberries**, **bilberries**, and **huckleberries**, lack this compound and don't keep well. They are, however, the most immediately consumable fruits in this genus, being delicious raw or cooked. Further, they provide an excellent source of a range of vitamins, minerals, and antioxidants. Leaf decoctions have been used as a gargle for inflammation of the mouth and throat.

Stinging nettles. East Sussex, UK.

Bilberry (European blueberry). Norbotten, Sweden.

Cowberry (Lingon). Norbotten, Sweden.

Yucca is a genus of plants in the asparagus family native to the Americas. Across the wide geographical areas they grow, **yuccas** are among the most important plants. Yucca leaves are a great source of fiber for cordage, basketry, woven matting, and even sandals. Dry flowering stems can be used for bow-drill and hand-drill friction fire. Yuccas are also the source of a traditional shampoo, produced by pounding the roots. In addition to the general uses, *Y. baccata*, **broadleaf yucca**, also known as banana yucca, produces fleshy edible fruit.

Banana yucca. Arizona, USA.

Narrowleaf yucca. Utah, USA.

THE ORIGINAL BUG SHIRT
ELITE EDITION

Procuring Fish and Small Game

Catching fish and small game are core skills for obtaining food from the land. All freshwater fish are edible. Small mammals such as rabbits, hares, and squirrels inhabit many parts of the world. The same goes for ground-feeding birds such as grouse, pheasants, and guinea fowl. Thus, knowledge of how to catch them is widely applicable.

Small game is more numerous than large game, which increases your chances of obtaining a meal. Small animals are easier to restrain and dispatch than large animals. They can be caught with simple, lightweight, portable equipment, some of which can be improvised easily. Once caught, small mammals, fowl, and fish do not need much butchery or processing. Nor might there be much excess beyond a meal. In this way, small game does not pose the problem of storage and preservation that large game does.

My assumption here, and in keeping with the philosophy of the rest of the material in this book, is that you wish to arrive in a spot and apply techniques directly. Fishing and small-game trapping can provide results literally overnight, if not immediately. Further, these techniques, and their yield, are more in keeping with the goals of those who are itinerant.

WHERE TO FISH

Fishing can be perceived as difficult, requiring technical equipment and arcane knowledge of fish species. This might be true if you are competition angling, or your aim is to land a record catch. The reality is you don't need much tackle or experience to start feeding yourself. It's true that the more you know about the behavior, habitat preferences, and feeding habits of a specific fish species, the more likely you are to land one of them. But remember, all freshwater fish are edible. Moreover, if you are fishing in areas that are not often fished, catching fish can be remarkably easy.

This all being said, there are some general observations and principles that will stand you in good stead.

Look for features that provide shelter for prey fish and offer ambush points for predatory fish. Footbridges are an obvious one, but also overhanging trees, reed beds, lily pads, and bank edges.

Fish obtain oxygen for respiration through their gills. So, fish are often attracted to areas with greater quantities of oxygenated water, such as near waterfalls, rapids, and weirs. Moving water is also likely to bring food to the fish. In rivers and streams, look for areas where faster-moving water meets slower-moving water—a seam or eddy line—since fish often congregate in these areas to conserve energy while still having access to food carried by the current. Fish can be attracted to areas where water enters or exits a lake or pond, such as small streams or drainage pipes, which bring in fresh oxygenated water and organic matter, including food.

Pay attention to what's occurring on the surface of the water. What is the availability of food sources such as fly hatches? Can you see any fish activity near types of flies on or near the surface? Sunrise and sunset are often the best times to fish, since fish tend to be more active and feed during these periods. If the water is relatively still, you'll start to see signs of fish rising, typically circular ripples on the surface.

More generally, at any time of day, observe fish activity by looking for signs of feeding, bubbles, fish jumping, or predatory fish chasing prey, which can include the chicks of water birds as well as other fish. Birds such as cormorants, mergansers, grebes, kingfishers, and herons can also serve as indicators of fish presence, since they prey on fish and reveal the locations of fish shoals.

Wind direction and air temperature play a role in fish location and fish activity. In the UK there are old sayings that contain some wisdom, such as *When the wind is in the west, the fish bite the best. When the wind is in the south, it blows the bait into the fish's mouth. When the wind is in the east, the fishes bite the least. When the wind is in the north, the fish don't go forth.* In the Northern Hemisphere, easterlies and northerlies are cold, while westerlies are milder and southerlies tend to be warm. The general principles are that fish don't like cold winds and are more active and feed better when there is a warm wind. Also, breezes will move food around the water. So, if you have a warm wind blowing onto shore, fishing near the shore is likely to be good, since the fish will be active, and this is where the fish will be feeding. In contrast, fish tend to move away from the shoreline during cold winds.

Water depth and water temperature are also factors, since different fish species have different preferences for these. If you are fishing at a particular depth with no success, try fishing either deeper or closer to the surface. Likewise, if you are using a particular type of lure or bait and, after a while of fishing, you have had no luck, change things up. Don't be impatient but do be prepared to vary what you are doing. Certainly, if you are angling, don't just keep making the same cast repeatedly. Cast into different areas of the water, closer in, farther out, walk along the bank or shoreline, and try a new spot.

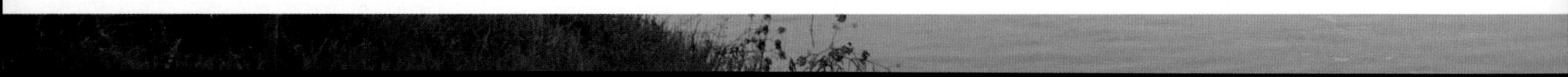

ACTIVE FISHING TECHNIQUES

Active fishing techniques are those where you are present with fishing equipment, working with the gear to hunt or attract fish and catch them. By contrast, passive fishing techniques (see page 164) are those that, once you have set up the equipment, you do something else while the fishing equipment catches fish for you. This is followed by you checking and collecting your catch later.

Active methods of fishing involving hooks will typically require some sort of bait, natural or artificial. If you are looking in the vicinity of your fishing spot for natural bait, then worms, maggots, grubs, and larvae are the best to go for first. The wrigglier the better. Slugs, deshelled snails, and grasshoppers can also work. Attractive berries or buds can sometimes work in gaining attention. For predatory fish such as pike, perch, and zander, using small, live, or dead fish—or parts of fish—can be attractive. For some fish, balls of dough or pieces of sweetcorn can also be effective. In even a small, minimalist fishing kit, you can carry brightly colored jigs, jellies, and small spoons and spinners for attracting fish.

Colorful jig heads combined with rubber jelly worms are easy to carry and versatile.

A classic five-of-diamonds spoon lure with a triple hook is very effective for predatory fish.

Handline Fishing

Handline fishing is a simple and effective method, especially useful in survival situations or when you are without a fishing rod but have minimal tackle. Essential gear includes monofilament fishing line, small hooks, split shot, and optionally, brightly colored weighted hooks or artificial lures.

A small amount of fishing gear can go a long way.

Making a Hobo Reel

Use a cylindrical object such as a bottle or can or carve one from wood. For a wooden reel, cut it 4–5 in. (10–13 cm) long, smooth the surface, and round the edges. Carve a small notch at one end to secure the line.

Setting Up the Reel

1. Attach the line: Tie an arbor knot around the cylinder or secure the line to a can's ring pull.
2. Wrap the line: Wind enough line for feasible casting. Avoid excess, since casting distance is limited by weight and technique. Heavier weights allow longer casts but disturb the water more.
3. Add the hook: Tie a hook to the line by using a secure knot, such as a half-blood knot.

Casting an improvised hand reel.

Casting and Retrieval

- Hold the reel in your nondominant hand and release a short length of line.
- Perform an underarm swing and release the line as it arcs toward the water. Point the reel end in the cast's direction to allow the line to run off smoothly.
- To retrieve, bring the reel across your body and wind the line back onto the cylinder.

Wooden hobo reel and catch.

Hand reels lack the control of rods, making it more challenging to play a fish, but they are surprisingly effective. Expect to catch smaller fish, such as brook trout, perch, rudd, or roach. While perch and brook trout are good eating, smaller fish such as roach can be used as bait for larger predators such as pike (see unattended lines on page 164).

How to Tie a Half-Blood Knot

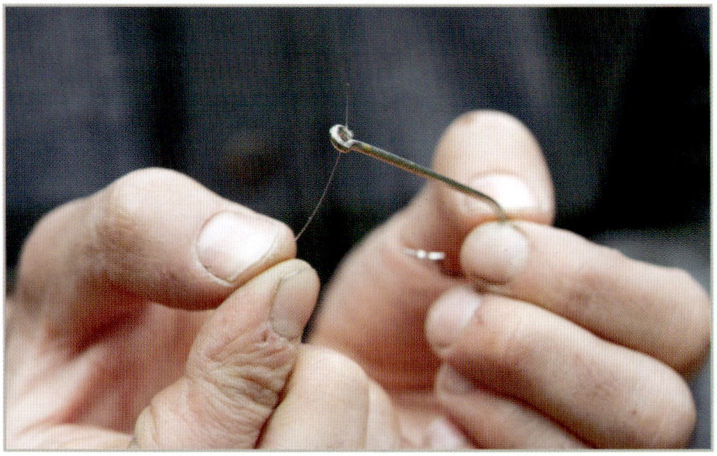

1. Feed the line through the eye of the hook.

2. *Pull through a good amount of line.*

3. *Rotate the hook so the line twists, with four to five turns.*

4. *Pass the end of the line through the loop you have created by twisting.*

5. *Grab the end of the line between your teeth.*

6. *Wet the knot in your mouth.*

7. *Pull the knot closed.*

8. *Ensure the knot is tight up against the hook.*

9. *Snip off the tag end.*

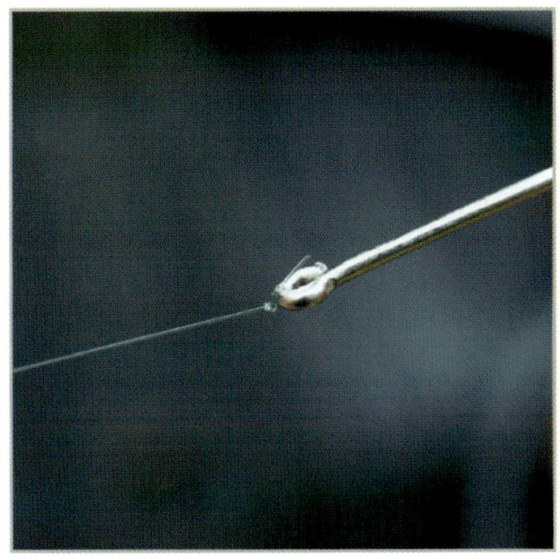

10. *Finished knot.*

Even in many wilderness areas, to be legal you need a rod and a fishing license.

Fishing with a Rod

In many places, even wild and remote areas, fishing with a rod is the only legal method of fishing, especially if you are not Indigenous. In many jurisdictions a rod license is required, plus there are catch limits. So, if we are fishing for leisure, to augment our supplies on a wilderness trip, perhaps, rather than for outright survival, we need to consider fishing rods.

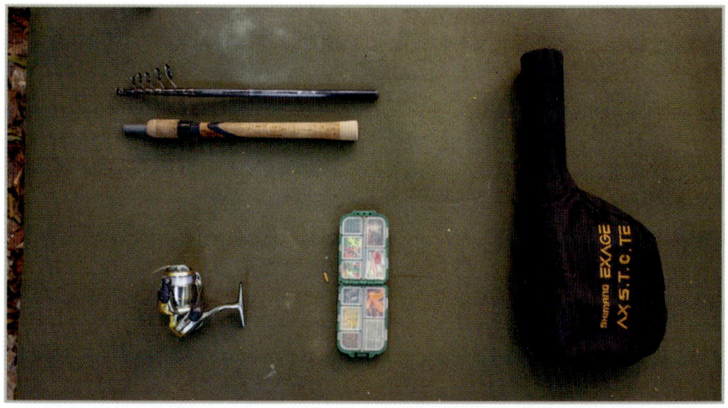

A compact but versatile spinning rod and tackle for travel.

Much of my perspective on equipment that integrates with bushcraft is based on my ability to take it to wild places. It needs to be portable and packable. Fortunately, there are travel rods available that break down to a size that can be carried in a backpack or a portage pack and stowed in a way they are not easily damaged.

The type of rod used for spinning, with an open reel, is probably the most versatile for travel. It's also the type that most people can get to grips with easily. A fly rod and reel is also an option but takes more time to learn how to use effectively because of the type of casting required.

A fly-fishing kit for travel.

Spinning rods and reels are versatile for freshwater fishing, especially if you are carrying light lures. Freshwater spinning rods tend to be quite light and flexible. A breakdown or telescopic spinning rod makes a good travel rod. This type of rod can be used with a range of lures such as spoons, jigs, spinners, and jellies or soft plastics. Whatever you can do with a hobo reel, you'll be much more effective with a rod-and-reel setup like this.

Fly Fishing

Fly fishing is a specialized method of freshwater fishing that involves using an artificial fly as bait to catch fish. The primary goal of fly fishing is to present the fly in a manner that imitates the natural movement and appearance of insects or other prey that fish feed on. Fly fishing is particularly popular for targeting species such as trout, salmon, and grayling. Fly fishing requires a specific set of gear and techniques.

If you are not already familiar with fly fishing, then trying to learn on your own on a wilderness trip is probably not the most fulfilling path. Going out with someone who can teach you a day at a time is the better approach. Lest you think that fly fishing is fussy or overly difficult, once someone is good at it, they can be incredibly effective at removing fish from the water.

Ice Fishing—Active

Ice fishing takes place on frozen lakes, ponds, and rivers, where ice has formed a thick and stable layer. It's something you might want to do when winter camping, especially if you are using waterways to travel on. A hole is created in the ice, using an ice auger or an ice chisel. While short fishing rods are regularly used for active ice fishing, it's possible to effectively ice-fish without a rod, using a hand reel, or work several holes with tip-up rigs that indicate when there is a bite. You can jig with a hand reel through the hole, using an artificial lure. This can work for lake trout or pike, for example. Small fish, minnows, smelt, or whitebait, used as dead bait will work better for pike.

Northern pike caught on a simple handline with a smelt as bait.

Ice fishing with a short rod. Ontario, Canada.

PASSIVE FISHING TECHNIQUES

Passive techniques are those that allow you to attend to other tasks, or rest, while the setup is (potentially) securing a catch for you. Unlike rod fishing, which tends to be treated similarly in many jurisdictions (allowed with a fishing license), passive techniques are subject to a lot more variation in how they are viewed. In some areas they are legal, while in others they are disallowed, even within the same country. Some techniques might require a special license or native rights to be employed legally. Check the local laws or regulations as to what is allowed in the area you might want to apply them. From a survival perspective, they are all valid.

Unattended Lines

The simplest version of a passive technique is an unattended line with a baited hook. Clearly the line needs to be secured such that any fish caught on the hook does not swim off with it. A line can be staked to the bank and the baited hook thrown out into the water. A float will prevent the hook sinking farther than you want it to. Tying off to a sapling can add some flex to the system, acting somewhat like a rod. Tying to an overhanging tree branch (limb lining) can allow a line to be set vertically into the water, with the bait held at a particular depth. With enough line, hooks, and bait, you can deploy multiple such lines. Make sure you mark them, so you remember where they are.

Slightly more complex is attaching multiple hooks to one line. The classic way of doing this is a trotline, where multiple hooked dropper lines are attached to a heavier main line at regular intervals. Droppers should be spaced such that they will not tangle with each other, even if both have a fish attached. The longer the dropper, the greater the spacing required.

The simplest trotlines can just be cheap nylon cord and hooks. Create overhand loops in the main line, then attach droppers to those loops. Overhand loops can be used to attach hooks to nylon cord and a cow hitch (see page 121) to attach the dropper to the loop on the main line.

In terms of what might be in a bushcraft bag, one could use paracord for a good amount of one of these setups. To make one for a stream or pond where you might be going for small fish, use a single strand of paracord inner as your main line. Use monofilament line as your droppers, each of which will have a small hook attached, using a half-blood knot. For larger fish you might want to make the main line from a full piece of paracord and the droppers from inner cord or from thicker, stronger monofilament.

Trotlines can be set in several ways. One way you see in diagrams in survival manuals is to set them at an angle from the surface of the water to the riverbed, the idea being the line fishes at different levels. It's nice in theory but can be very awkward to set. How do you attach it to the bed? Attaching it to a heavy weight, such as a large rock, will work to get it down there, but how do you retrieve it? More practical in many situations is to span the main line across a body of water, attaching each end to something that is accessible, such as overhanging branches. If you want to experiment with fishing at different levels because you don't know what is optimal for the species of fish present, you can easily vary the length of dropper hanging from a horizontal main line.

Ice Fishing—Passive

In regions where passive ice fishing is legal, you can set multiple static lines overnight. Dead small fish work well as bait, and thin twine is often used, though heavier monofilament is an option. To prevent the line from being cut when chipping frozen holes, attach it to the bottom of a stick inserted into the hole. Use a stick with a side branch shaped like a checkmark: Invert it and place the fork over a straight stick spanning the hole to secure the setup and control fishing depth. To minimize ice formation, add green spruce to the hole and cover it with a mound of snow for insulation. Mark the mound with a stick to locate it later.

Burbot caught while ice fishing in Sweden.

Fish Traps

Fish traps vary in size and shape. The fundamental idea, however, is that fish can easily enter the trap, then find it difficult to exit. Typically, this is achieved by funneling a fish toward a narrow aperture to enter the trap, with no such guidance for the fish on the interior of the trap's enclosure.

Many traditional fish traps have much in common with basketry of the area they were made, both in terms of materials used and construction techniques. A common design, found in many parts of the world, is a cylindrical enclosure with an inverted cone at the entrance. A similar effect can be created by cutting off the angled top section of a plastic soda bottle, inverting it, and placing it inside the cylindrical part of the bottle. Traditional traps are typically larger, but plastic bottle traps can be useful for catching small bait fish for use with other techniques. The top section of a bottle trap should be fixed in place with wooden pegs or short pieces of cordage passed through both pieces of plastic.

Ideally, fish traps should be baited with something that has good scent, even bread, which will encourage fish into them. If you place a fish trap into a flowing stream or river, position it so the entrance is on the downstream side.

Conical entrance of a traditional cylindrical fish trap.

A traditional Swahili coast dema basket fish trap.

Netting

While netting fish can be an active pursuit—using cast nets, seine nets, or drag nets, for example—static netting using a gill net is a particularly effective method of passive fishing. A gill net is a rectangular net that is suspended in water so that a wall of netting is presented. Fish swim into the net, going partway through before becoming stuck due to the gauge of the net not allowing any further progress. Then they cannot get back out since their gills become caught. As they struggle, they tend to become more entangled still. The mesh size determines the size of fish caught, with smaller fish being able to pass through. Gill nets will catch a wider range of species than you would catch by angling with a particular tackle setup or type of bait. In this sense, gill nets are indiscriminate. They are also typically very efficient, catching a significant number of fish in a relatively short space of time. If I could have only one piece of survival fishing equipment, it would be a gill net.

If the net is relatively small, say only a few yards across, then I would try to find a smaller channel or constriction to set the net across. A larger net can be set out from the bank of a lake, attached at the shore, and anchored out in the water. Given the size of the nets and potential depth of water, the easiest way to set such a net is from a boat, canoe, or raft. Otherwise, the method is to swim the net out. Another good placement of a gill net can be parallel to the outside edge of a reed bed, where fish are darting in and out of cover. This is much easier to set up with some sort of watercraft.

A First Nations friend sets a gill net from a boat. Ontario, Canada.

Gill nets will catch a range of species.

IMPROVISED FISHING EQUIPMENT

There are a few potentially useful pieces of improvised fishing equipment that are quick and easy to create. The first is to create a wire leader for catching predatory fish that are apt to sever monofilament (for example pike). This can be used with a static line, hobo reel, or rod.

Making an Improvised Wire Leader

Use 0.3mm–0.5mm brass or stainless steel wire from your kit. Cut a 12in (30cm) length. Double the wire without kinking it, aligning the ends. Insert one end ½in (1.25cm) through the hook's eye, bend it back, and repeat with the other end in the opposite direction. Twist the four wires so they come together and retain the hook.

Now snag the hook on a stable wooden object such as a log. Insert an ⅛in (4–5mm) diameter tapered stick at the other end as a toggle. Twist the toggle to entwine the wire strands, matching the hook's twist direction to avoid undoing it. Use your fingers to smooth and even the twists. Stop when you achieve a neat, uniform twist without overtightening.

An improvised leader made from brass snare wire.

Making Improvised Hooks

I start this with a caveat: In some parts of the world there is little, or no evidence of small fish hook use before contact with Europeans. Traditional methods of catching fish were often trapping, netting, spearing, and natural fish poisons.

Gorge Hooks

Gorge hooks are ancient, straight fishing hooks used for thousands of years, often made from bone, wood, or cactus spines. Unlike modern hooks, they lack curve or barb.

The hook is hidden in bait, with the line tied at its middle. When swallowed, it rotates horizontally in the fish's throat or gut. Gently pulling the line sets the hook, allowing the angler to retrieve the fish. To make a gorge hook, select a small, straight piece of bone, hardwood, or similar material. Carve it into a straight or slightly tapered shape with sharpened ends, ensuring it's strong enough to hold a fish.

While gorge hooks can be valuable in certain situations, especially in survival situations, they have some disadvantages compared to modern hooks. Gorge hooks can be more challenging to use, as they require the fish to swallow the bait entirely.

Thorn Hooks

While not as durable or consistent as metal hooks, natural hooks can still be effective. Thorns from species such as hawthorn, blackthorn, or honey locust can be used as hooks due to their naturally sharp points on side shoots. Select a section of twig, with a sharp side shoot or thorn, looking to preserve a checkmark-shaped piece. Secure fishing line or natural cordage to the main shank. Carve a small groove if needed to hold the line in place.

Gorge hook and thorn hooks.

TRAPPING: LEGAL AND ETHICAL CONSIDERATIONS

Trapping should never be done for fun. Traps cause death, and sometimes pain. If a trap is designed to catch rather than kill, it can still cause physical injury, as well as certainly causing stress. Anyone considering trapping an animal should be clear-eyed about the consequences, including the potential for having to dispatch an animal caught in a trap. The taking of any life should not be done lightly. It should be approached with seriousness and with the utmost respect for the animal. We must be as humane as possible. If we are successful, we should be grateful and make good use of the catch, avoiding being wasteful. Under normal circumstances, we should also follow the law in the jurisdiction within which we are operating. Laws and ethical considerations are not the same thing, or perfectly aligned. It's my belief our ethics should be the higher standard.

Many types of traditional traps are illegal in many countries, or territories within them, while in some places they are still allowed and even used to this day by Indigenous peoples who maintain traditional lifeways. Further, some modern trapping techniques, or at least trapping techniques that employ modern materials, are illegal in numerous jurisdictions. In jurisdictions where they are allowed, their use is often controlled or licensed. It's said, somewhat glibly in many cases, that if you want to know which trapping techniques are effective, just look at what is illegal. I don't believe it is as simple as this.

Some techniques are effective, still legal but hardly used. In the lifetime of some professional gamekeepers I have worked with, they have gone from setting hundreds of snares to control the numbers of nonnative rabbits, to using silenced .22 rimfire rifles at night with the aid of powerful spotlights, often from the back of a quad bike or ATV. The latter approach, involving more-modern technology, is more time efficient, cost effective, and discriminate. Going further back in time, after being introduced to wire, many First Nations groups quickly moved from setting snares of plant fiber cordage or rawhide—attached to tip-up mechanisms, sprung saplings, or tossing logs—to attaching a wire loop directly to a solid object. A rabbit can't chew through brass wire. Again, the more modern technology allowed for greater efficiency in time and effort. But this did not negate the effectiveness of the older techniques.

Concern for animal welfare has certainly been a driving force for the restriction or banning of some techniques. Environmental concerns and conservation efforts also play a significant role in the treatment of trapping, particularly in sensitive habitats, national parks, conservation areas, and the like. In particular, it's imperative to avoid trapping endangered species, even by accident. Further, the presence of domesticated livestock, gamebirds, and pets in some areas has been a factor in making traps less desirable. Traps can be indiscriminate, especially if set by those who are not experienced. As such, they can kill or cause injury to nontarget species. If placed incorrectly, a simple wire rabbit snare will kill a hedgehog or catch or kill a pheasant, for example; further, it can catch a larger animal such as a deer by the leg, or even a cow by the tongue. Whether or not a certain type of trap is illegal in a particular place, you must, as part of your ethical considerations, think about unintended potential outcomes and avoid them.

Further, we should make a distinction between trapping for food, trapping for fur, and trapping to control numbers. My primary interest in trapping is its potential to provide food, and I think this is the core reason to have some aptitude in trapping. It's worth noting that trapping for food is not subject to a legal landscape defined purely by consideration for animal welfare or the wider environment. Populations that can feed themselves from the land are harder to control. Those in authority have long had a vested interest in removing this level of independence from the general populace. This has been done through removing people from their traditional lands, restricting access to large swathes of country, limiting hunting rights for all but the elite, making specific trapping or hunting techniques illegal, restricting access to specialized equipment, or making its possession illegal.

In the modern day, however, I completely understand why, from a purely ethical stance, a reader may have no interest in this chapter, or employing anything contained here. I very much respect this level of principle. There's also a middle road, which is to learn the techniques but not use them. Learning trap mechanisms can be fascinating. The ingenuity of some traps is remarkable, as is the simplicity of some of them. My personal stance is that I'd rather know how to do something and not need it, than to need it and not know how to do it.

The author with a snowshoe hare, northern Ontario, Canada.

TRAPPING SMALL MAMMALS

From the snowshoe hare of the boreal forests to the scrub hare of southern Africa, rabbits share similar habits and can be trapped using similar methods. Squirrels are also abundant, as are mice, which inhabit nearly every country.

Health Precautions

Handling small mammals may expose you to bacteria and viruses:
Tularemia: Caused by *Francisella tularensis*, spread via damaged skin, mucous membranes, or inhalation. Found in rabbits and rodents, primarily in North America and less commonly in Europe.
Plague: Caused by *Yersinia pestis*, with rodents as reservoirs and fleas as vectors. Present in Asia, sub-Saharan Africa, and western USA.
Leptospirosis: Spread through animal urine, droppings, or contaminated water, entering through mucous membranes or broken skin. Severe cases are known as Weil's disease.
Hantaviruses: Transmitted through rodent urine, droppings, or saliva, especially via inhalation. Found worldwide, these viruses can cause severe illness.
To minimize risk, wear nitrile gloves when handling carcasses, protect cuts, disinfect tools, and wash hands thoroughly after working with raw meat. Dispose of entrails away from camp and water sources. Avoid disturbing rodent nests or inhaling dust in areas with high rodent activity.

Snow hare tracks and dropping. Norbotten, Sweden.

Gray squirrel feeding midden. East Sussex, UK.

Where to Set Traps

Start by figuring out where the animals are active. This can be through direct observation of animals in an area. More often, though, areas of regular animal activity will be detected by concentrations of tracks, feeding sign, and droppings. Look out for tracks and sign of other animals in the same vicinity, so you can avoid setting traps in places where it might endanger nontarget species.

Mushroom placed in tree by a squirrel. Ontario, Canada.

There's lots of small rodent activity under a rock overhang. Arizona, USA.

Clear small animal trail through lichen. Saskatchewan, Canada.

Snaring

Snaring with brass wire is a relatively simple method of trapping that can be effective in providing food. It requires little equipment. Even if snaring is legal in the territory you wish to apply it, before you go onto the land you must research exactly what is allowed and what is not. How the snare is constructed, the gauge of wire used, the size of the loop, and how the snare is secured can all be stipulated in regulations.

Rabbit Snares

Rabbit means different things in different territories. In my home country, rabbit means the European brown rabbit, *Oryctolagus cuniculus*, which has been introduced more widely, including Australia. In North America, rabbit can mean any one of several species, including cottontail rabbits in the genus *Sylvilagus*, and jackrabbits, in the genus *Lepus*. The latter are hares. The snowshoe hare, or varying hare, *Lepus americanus*, found primarily in boreal regions of North America, is also referred to as a rabbit.

Rabbit snaring, then, does not involve one species, and there is not one uniform method. There are also varying rules and regulations. In some regions the practice is to use a single strand of wire of a specified gauge, while in others a multistranded wire snare is stipulated. Making multistranded snares is not something to be done out on the trapline. You should prepare a batch of them ahead of placing them. Below is a method for making a multistranded rabbit snare with a free-running eyelet that (at the time of writing) is legal in England and Wales. More generally, it is a good method to know for making a snare that is strong yet malleable.

Multistranded Rabbit Snares

To make this type of snare in batches, it's worth making a couple of tools. The first is creating a simple jig. Take a straight piece of timber and add two panel tacks, spaced for the desired snare length. For a European rabbit, a snare of diameter about 6½ in. (16.5 cm) is good. This translates to placing your tacks 20 in. (50 cm) apart. The second is some sort of weighty spinner. A gamekeeper I used to work with used a cast-iron wheel from an old train station porter's trolley with a tent peg welded into the center. In a base camp in the woods, I use a green log and some fencing wire. The latter resembles a heavyweight coat hanger.

To create multistranded snares, use 25-gauge wire. This has a diameter of just under 0.5 mm. You'll also need some brass eyelets. We're also going to make a peg and tealer stick for each snare so they can be set up in meadows, open understory, and the like, without needing to tie off to trees or logs.

Step 1: Forming the Snare on the Jig

1. Place a brass eyelet onto one of the tacks on your jig.
2. Pull out a length of brass wire and bend the first ¾ in. (2 cm) around the top of the eyelet.
3. Pull the wire down to the second tack, loop it back to the first tack, and repeat until you have six strands (three full circuits).
4. Cut the wire, leaving a ¾ in. (2 cm) tail. Bend this over the top of the eyelet.

Step 2: Twisting the Snare

1. At the eyelet end, remove the snare from the jig while holding the strands and eyelet together.
2. Twist the eyelet into the strands so everything binds together.
3. Remove the other end of the snare from the jig and hang your heavy spinner from that end.
4. Spin the spinning tool in the correct direction to put twists in the same direction at the eyelet end.
5. Run your hand up and down the snare length to ensure even distribution of the twists.

Eyelet end removed from the jig and twisted together.

Using the spinning tool to twist the strands together.

Step 3: Form the Snare Loop

1. Take the noneyelet end and pass it through the eyelet to form the loop.
2. Open out the noneyelet end so it does not pull back through the eyelet.
3. The memory of the wire being straight will keep the loop in a nice shape.
4. Take a 2 ft. (60 cm) length of paracord, double it over, then pass the bight through the wire loop at the end without the eyelet.
5. Form a lark's foot (see page 121) by pulling the tails through the cord loop and over the brass.

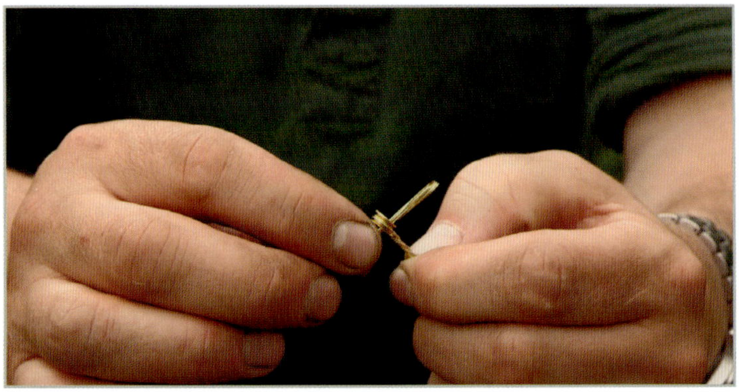

Forming the loop by passing the plain end through the eyelet.

Step 4: Make a Peg and Attach It

1. Making a snare peg is very similar to a tarp peg. Choose a straight stick 10–12 in. (25–30 cm) long, about the thickness of your thumb knuckle.
2. Carve a three-sided point at one end.
3. Bevel the top to prevent splitting when hammered.
4. Create a shallow notch below the top by making a stop cut and shaving toward it. This helps secure the cord and is very important.
5. Take the two strands of paracord and tie them together with an overhand knot (see page 118) about 4 in. (10 cm) from the ends.
6. Butt this stopper up against the peg and take a strand on either side of the peg, around the back, and tie together on the snare side, not the backside of the peg.

Step 5: Make a Tealer Stick

1. Take a stick that's about pencil thickness and 8–10 in. (20–25 cm) long (you can shorten it later if necessary).
2. Point one end and chamfer the other.
3. Put a split in the chamfered end like a mini candlestick holder.

Step 6: Setting the Snare

1. Locate a rabbit run.
2. Place the snare between two hop spots where rabbits frequently travel.
3. Drive the peg firmly into the ground to secure the snare.
4. Insert the wire (not the cord) into the split in the tealer stick. Pull it back to the knot for a secure grip. Push the tealer into the ground to suspend the snare. I do this at an angle to keep the tealer away from the trail.
5. Position the snare loop at the correct height: four fingers and an upturned thumb from the ground.
6. Ensure the loop is not kinked and fully open.
7. Make sure you mark the position of the snare so you can retrieve it.

Snare set on a rabbit trail in long grass, with angled tealer and peg firmly anchored.

Even in open grassland, snares are hard to see.

Dispatching a Rabbit

Snares with free-running eyelets as described above tend to catch and hold rabbits rather than kill them. So if you set them, you should be prepared to find a live rabbit in the snare and be able to dispatch it quickly. The best way to do this is quickly break the rabbit's neck while it is still in the snare.

Approach the rabbit and put both your hands firmly onto its back. Slide one hand toward its head (keeping fingers away from its mouth) and slide the other hand along its hind quarters and take control of its strong back legs. Now, holding the neck below the head with your thumb and fingers, pull the back legs vertically up while cranking the neck. You will feel the neck crack and it will be over quickly.

The position to achieve cervical dislocation. This can be done with the rabbit still in a snare.

Single-Strand Rabbit Snares

We'll use snowshoe hares as an example here. 22-to-24-gauge wire is recommended for single-strand snares for these animals. It's easy enough to make a snare in the wilderness, but in cold conditions you might want to make some before you head out. Keep the length quite long, since you will not be using a tealer but attaching the wire directly to a fixed object in the forest. Take a small twig about ⅛ in. (3 mm) in diameter, wrap the wire around the stick, and then twist the stick like a toggle to wind the wire around itself. This creates the eyelet. Feed the free end of wire through the eyelet.

To set your snares, look for natural choke points, or obstacles the hares will have to pass under. As another option, you can take a dead tree and lay it at an angle to create this setup. Natural chokes are helpful, and you can use additional twigs for fencing to further channel the rabbits into the snares.

Single-strand snare.

A clear snowshoe hare trail leading under an obstacle has been snared.

Snowshoe hare caught and killed by simple single-strand snare.

Squirrel Snares

You can use the same brass wire as your rabbit snares. I use 25 gauge.

Step 1: Cut a length of wire on the basis of the pole diameter (see squirrel poles below). Avoid excessive length, since shorter tails ensure better positioning and rigidity. Keep the wire straight. Prevent kinks during handling.

Step 2: Form an eyelet. Tie an overhand knot near one end of the wire. Leave a tail of about ½–¾ in. (1–2 cm) for security. Gently cinch the knot to form a small, fixed loop.

Step 3: Shape the snare. Pass the opposite end of the wire through the eyelet to create the adjustable loop. Ensure the loop is free of kinks and can slide smoothly.

Step 4: Determining loop size. For American gray squirrels, a three-finger-wide loop is recommended. For smaller squirrel species, a two-to-three-finger loop width is appropriate.

Squirrel snare eyelet detail.

Squirrel Pole

Squirrels are fantastic climbers, easily ascending a tree trunk vertically. They will still take advantage of easier routes up off the ground, though. This is the idea with a squirrel pole. Set them in areas where you see squirrels active on the ground or at least see evidence of them feeding on the ground.

Choose a straight pole approximately 12 ft. (3.6 m) long with a diameter of 1–2 in. (2.5–5 cm) at the thin end. Avoid heavy, thick poles. Thin poles are preferable, since they limit the squirrel's ability to climb along the sides. The poles can be green, dead standing, or anything in between. Trim off any side branches to create a clean surface. Lean the pole against a tree at an angle of 45 to 60 degrees.

Attach the snare to the pole by twisting the wire tail securely around it. The attachment should be tight enough to hold the snare in place but not so tight that it kinks the wire. Depending on the size of the target species, ensure the snare loops are positioned about one to two fingers above the pole's surface.

If you place multiple snares on the same pole, ensure they are spaced far enough apart to avoid entanglement. Contrary to many survival manuals, don't set them at different angles. Rather, align the snares so that they form a clear path or tube when viewed from the bottom of the pole. This is much better than presenting the squirrel with a tangled mess.

Additionally, the plane of each snare loop should be perpendicular to the pole's long axis. Avoid placing snares too close to the ground or tree trunk, since this could allow the squirrel to gain leverage and escape.

Position the pole in areas with visible signs of squirrel activity, such as middens or feeding sites. If time permits, consider setting up poles several days in advance without snares. This allows squirrels to become accustomed to the poles as part of their environment, increasing your chances of success when snares are eventually added.

Humane dispatch of trapped squirrels is essential. If a squirrel is caught but still alive, use a sturdy stick to strike its head before removing it from the snare. Never handle a live squirrel directly, since they can give a nasty bite with their sharp, chisel-like teeth.

Squirrel pole against a tree.

Squirrel snare set on a pole.

Deadfall Traps

Generally, these traps are made entirely from natural materials. They don't always take long to fashion but can take a bit of skill to make them work properly, so are bush*craft*. Constructing the trigger mechanisms will improve your carving skills. There are very few places where deadfall traps can be used legally. In terms of their modern-day application, these mechanisms sit at the survival skills end of the spectrum, reserved for use in emergencies when gloves are off. I would recommend making some as an exercise, though, so that you can make them work rather than having only theoretical knowledge.

Figure 4

There are multiple variants of this idea. The fundamental concept of the trap trigger is that there is an upright stick, broken in the middle, which is holding up a weighty object. The reason the stick does not fold at the break is the horizontal trigger stick, which precariously holds everything together. If there is a trick with figure 4 trap mechanisms, it's ensuring the three parts of the trigger collapse once the trigger stick has been disturbed. In particular, the trigger stick must fall free of the upright.

Deadfall trap with figure 4 trigger.

Trigger detail. Note the scallop in the upright so the trigger falls offline once disturbed.

Paiute deadfall set for mice.

Checking and Removing Traps

Don't fall into the temptation of checking traps too often. All you will do is cause disturbance. Equally, if you leave them too long, you may provide an easy meal for a predator or scavenger. Rabbits and mice are more active at night. Check traps after first light. Tree squirrels are busy during the day, so check toward the end of the day.

When you have finished trapping in an area, it is imperative you remove all your traps. Start out with this in mind. Mark your traps so you can find them.

Another variant on the figure 4 mechanism.

Paiute Deadfall

The so-called Paiute deadfall is named after the Paiute people, traditionally a highly mobile hunting and gathering people of the Great Basin. This trap is an amalgam of ingenious ideas. It bears some superficial resemblance to figure 4 mechanisms but, unlike these, does not require much carving prowess. It does, however, require some good-quality natural cordage.

This trap consists of a heavy object, such as a rock or log, balanced on a simple five-part wooden trigger mechanism made from a base stick, vertical post, horizontal lever stick, trigger stick, and cordage with toggle. Bait is attached to the trigger stick, which holds the toggle precariously in place. When the bait is disturbed, the trigger releases, causing the deadfall to collapse and crush the prey.

TRAPPING BIRDS

Here the focus is on trapping *ground-feeding* birds such as grouse, ptarmigan, guinea fowl, pheasants, and the like. They regularly come down into our domain or even spend much of the time on the ground, where they leave tracks and feeding signs. Many of them don't like to fly very far, if at all. Thcy tend to be relatively heavy, with a good amount of meat on them. Trapping them is still legal in some places, and the materials required are very similar to what you would use for small mammals.

Wire Snares

Some species of ground-feeding birds can be snared with wire snares oriented vertically, very similar to rabbit snaring. Indeed, pheasants or grouse are sometimes found in rabbit snares. But to successfully target them, you need to know where the birds are likely to be walking. If there are defined routes through, or around, a feature, where you can see the birds are transiting, this will be possible. Also, if you know what the birds like to feed on, you can set traps accordingly, in terms of location and bait.

Equally, you can create routes or openings for the birds. This is exactly how ptarmigan snaring is taught (and tested) in Sweden before trappers gain their ptarmigan-snaring license. A fence of food is constructed, with openings in the fence for birds to pass through, the openings being snared with fine (0.3 mm) stainless-steel wire. The fence is built from green birch sticks with winter buds on them, placed upright in the snow, so that the birds can walk along the fence feeding on the buds, just as they do on small birches. There must be snow on the ground to employ this method. Similar techniques were also used in Canada for ptarmigan and other grouse, with the set looking like a somewhat smaller version of what was used for rabbits. Again, such snares were not set in summer.

Ptarmigan tracks heading toward small birch trees. Agder, Norway.

Some species of wild birds such as spruce grouse can seem remarkably indifferent to the presence of humans, or even curious. In some parts they are referred to as fool hens. On wilderness canoe trips in Canada, I've had them come right into my camp. In the past, people would certainly have chanced throwing a rock or stout stick to stun one. Even when they are spooked, these birds usually fly up onto a tree branch and sit there. One method of catching a tree bird is to attach a snare to the end of a long pole. Slowly bring the loop in front of the bird, then pull sharply over the bird's head toward the body before the bird has time to react. I've also read old poacher's tales of taking roosting pheasants in a similar fashion.

Male spruce grouse behind the author's overnight camp. Ontario, Canada.

Female spruce grouse perched in a tree. Manitoba, Canada.

Bushman Bird Snare

What follows is a modern, and more generally applicable, take on a bird snare employed by bushmen of the Kalahari. This trap can be employed to catch a variety of ground-feeding birds, including guinea fowl, pheasants, larger grouse, and even chickens. The idea is to create a space into which the bird must put its head to reach food. By pecking at bait on the trap's trigger stick, the noose will be released and tightened around the bird's neck. The trap won't necessarily kill the bird, but it will certainly tether it. The original design of this trap involves digging a hole in firm, dry earth with little or no coverage of foliage or leaf litter. The dug hole creates the aperture into which the target species (guinea fowl, originally) must place its head. In the version below, I create the aperture by suspending the cordage above the ground.

Guinea fowl feeding. Limpopo, South Africa.

Here I am using paracord, on the assumption that most modern bushcrafters will have some. Key qualities of any cordage used is that it's strong and slides freely. Traditionally, natural cordage made from *Sansevieria* leaf fibers was used. *Yucca* leaf fibers would also be a good option. Natural cordage needs to be tightly twisted, then polished to run smoothly.

1. *Find a flexible sapling in a suitable location. Remove green leaves to reduce drag.*

2. *For positioning the trap, locate the area of ground directly under the bent sapling.*

3. *Take a wand of green, flexible wood, sharpen the ends, and insert them into the ground to make an inverted U-shaped hoop.*

4. *Tie paracord to the sapling, bend it over, and note the point where the cord meets the ground hoop. This is where you'll tie in a toggle.*

5. *Make a small toggle that will fit between the hoop and the ground.*

6. *Tie the toggle into the cord, using a clove hitch (see page 120). Note it is tied off-center.*

7. *Source a forked trigger stick and take it under the hoop, bringing its end past the toggle. Then push it the other way so the end digs into the ground.*

8. *With the end of the trigger stick firmly embedded into the ground, allow the toggle to come to meet it at the end, so the trigger stick is put under pressure. This is a bit fiddly, and the trigger stick may need to be shortened or reembedded farther away, or even closer.*

9. *Create a slipped overhand knot with an overhand stopper at the end. It should have sufficient diameter to extend from the toggle to a good distance beyond the trigger stick.*

10. *Suspend the noose above the ground and the trigger stick with small, forked sticks. Note the noose does not extend onto the toggle, since you do not want the toggle springing up into the noose, preventing it from tightening.*

11. *For safety while setting the trap, keep your face out of the arc of the sprung sapling.*

12. *Bring local ground cover materials around the raised loop of cord so that the only way the target species can access food inside is by placing its head in the noose. The side branch on the trigger stick should be baited with food attractive to the bird.*

GAME PREPARATION

Once you have caught a fish, small mammal, or bird, you need to prepare it for cooking. A knife is useful for some of this work. As a general point, when cutting raw meat or fish, to avoid the introduction of bacteria, don't return your knife to its sheath until it has been washed or disinfected.

Preparing Fish

Gutting a Fish

Cleaning a fish is straightforward. All the innards are contained in one cavity. Some people will remove the jaw at the same time as the guts. I like to leave it on if I am going to cook the fish on a stick over the fire.

1. Invert your knife and start a shallow incision at the vent (anus), continuing up the belly to behind the gills. If there are eggs inside, you can choose to set these aside for eating.

2. Grab the entrails and pull them all out, including the swim bladder. The cavity should now be clean apart from the kidney, which runs along underneath the spine behind a membrane.

3. Scrape out the kidney with your thumbnail or the tip of a knife. Give the fish a rinse to remove the material.

4. Insert a green stick and cook over a fire.

1. Starting the incision.

2. Continue to behind the jaw.

3. Pull out the entrails.

4. *The cavity should now be clean.*

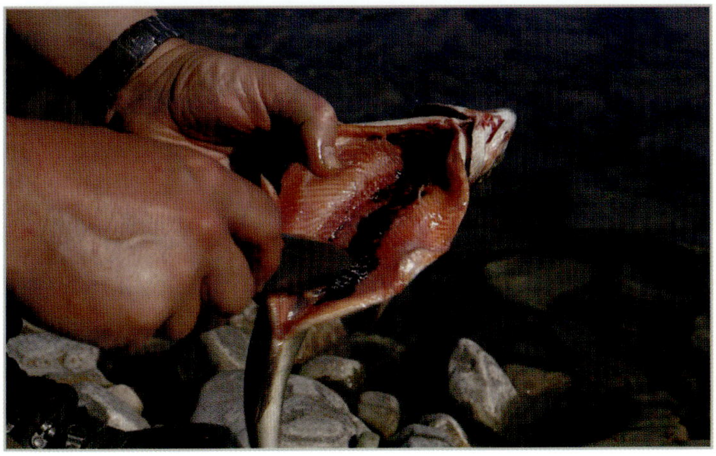

5. *Scraping out the kidney.*

6. *Inserting a green stick.*

7. *Cooking over a fire.*

Filleting a Fish

Smaller fish can be gutted then cooked directly over the fire, grilled, or pan-fried. Larger fish are more likely to require filleting, so that you can cook the flesh properly. It also removes most, if not all, of the bones. The following method works with many fish species.

1. Lay the fish flat, then locate the pectoral fin on the fish's side, behind its head. Place the knife just behind the fin, angled toward the head. Cut down firmly through the skin and scales until you hit the backbone. Stop there.

2. Starting near the head, make a shallow incision along the spine and parallel to the edge of the dorsal fin on the fish's back. Use short, controlled strokes, cutting approximately 1.5 in. (4 cm) deep.

3. Once your cut along the back is opposite the anal opening, push the knife through to the other side of the fish. This avoids the ribcage (and entrails if they are still in the fish).

4. Cut toward the tail, then slice through the skin just before the tail so the fillet becomes free at the tail end.

5. Starting at the tail end, lift the fillet and slice forward toward the head, working along the ribs. Follow the contour of the ribs, listening for a light clicking sound as your knife moves over them.

6. Once past the ribs, angle the knife back down and cut away the belly meat. Remove the fillet, leaving the skin intact. This fillet can be pan-fried or grilled as it is, but if you want to remove the skin, proceed as follows.

7. Hold the skin firmly and cut under the flesh so the knife is parallel to the skin. Angle your knife slightly so it doesn't cut into the skin. Then use a smooth sawing motion to separate the skin from the meat. Move steadily along the fillet as you slice.

8. To remove any remaining pin bones, lay the skinned fillet flat and feel along the centerline for the bones. Make a shallow cut on either side of the bones, as close as possible to minimize wastage. Remove the pin bones strip, leaving a completely boneless fillet.

1. First cut. (Ray Goodwin)

2a. Start at the head. (Ray Goodwin)

2b. Cut alongside the dorsal fin. (Ray Goodwin)

3. Once in line with the anus, push the knife all the way through. (Ray Goodwin)

4. Now cut along to the tail. (Ray Goodwin)

5. Then work back toward the head. (Ray Goodwin)

6. Finally, cut away the belly meat. (Ray Goodwin)

7. A detached fillet. (Ray Goodwin)

8. Removing the flesh from the skin. Some flex in the knife helps. (Ray Goodwin)

Preparing Small Mammals

Skinning, Gutting, and Jointing a Rabbit

Step 1: Empty the Bladder

Hold the rabbit vertically with its hind legs downward. Squeeze the rabbit's abdomen gently to empty the bladder. A few firm strokes down the belly toward its groin should do the job.

Step 2: Skinning the Rabbit

1. **Make the initial incision:** Pull the belly skin taut and make a small horizontal cut through the skin, avoiding the guts beneath.
2. **Separate the skin:** Work your fingers under the skin on either side of the incision, then to the back so the skin is separated all the way around the middle of the animal.
3. **Divide the skin:** Rip the skin apart with your hands, dividing it into top and bottom. With tough buck rabbits, you may need your knife to cut the skin once separated.
4. **Remove the skin:**
   - Pull the bottom down over the rump and legs.
   - Pull the top up over the front legs and head, working it off the elbows by hooking a finger under each joint.
5. **Remove the head:** Once the fur is up over the head, twist the neck to break it to detach the head.

Cut only the skin.

Work the top half over the elbows.

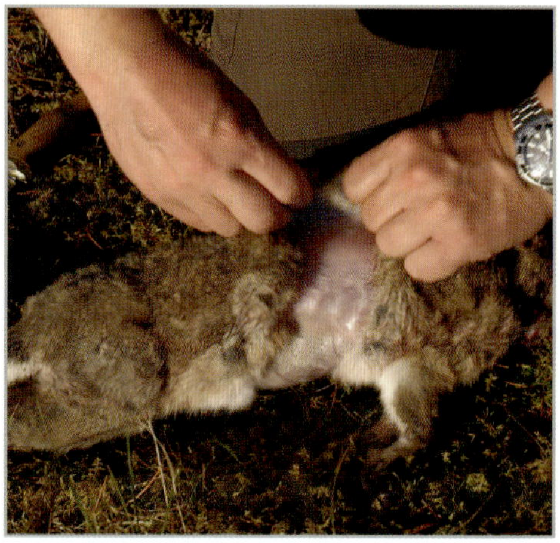

Rip the skin all the way round.

Pull the top half up over the head, then twist to remove the head.

Pull off the bottom half.

Step 3: Gutting the Rabbit

Gutting can be done with the fur on, or after taking the fur off.

1. Make a small horizontal cut across the belly, being careful not to puncture organs.
2. Open the cavity by pulling with your fingers.
3. Holding the rabbit vertically, scoop out the entrails, which are attached only at the top (esophagus) and bottom (rectum), using gravity to help them fall out of the body cavity.
4. Inspect the liver for marbling or white spots, which indicate disease (e.g., myxomatosis). The liver should look healthy, and if it is, it can be consumed.
5. Remove the heart and lungs by pushing up through the diaphragm with your fingers and scooping behind the ribs. The heart is small, but it can be eaten.
6. The kidneys will be attached to the inside of the body, about the size of a butterbean. Remove them and set them aside.
7. Check the pelvis for droppings, using your pinky finger to push any out.

Pull the flesh away from the guts and cut horizontally.

Rip the thin flesh to open up the cavity.

Step 4: Removing the Legs and Tail

If you have a heavier cutting tool such as a hatchet or a machete, you can simply amputate the feet above where there is any remaining fur. Otherwise, break the relevant joints by hand by locking them straight, then applying lateral pressure.

1. **Back legs:** Break the hock joint, then cut through the tendons and ligaments to detach the legs.
2. **Front legs:** Break the wrist joint, then slice through the connective tissue.
3. **Remove the tail:** You can often pull off the bulk of the tail fur with your finger and thumb. If it is resistant, cut around the tail base, then pull.

Step 5: Jointing the Rabbit

1. **Saddle:** On both sides, insert your knife in front of the hip bone, then slice diagonally back until you hit the spine. With the tip of your knife, cut across the top of the spine and across the inside of the spine. Now snap the spine back and forward to remove the hind quarters, setting them aside. Next, holding the saddle, cut behind the last rib, running your knife parallel to the rib until you hit the spine. Do this on both sides and cut across the spine inside and out. Now snap the spine again to separate the saddle from the ribs, with the front legs attached.
2. **Front legs and shoulder:** There is no real shoulder joint, only connective tissue. Hold a front leg, letting the weight of the ribs stretch out the flesh. Cut around the meat as close to the ribs as possible. Do the same with the other leg.
3. **Haunches:** Find the ball-and-socket joint in the pelvis. Cut across the inside of the leg to expose the actual ball and socket. Now carefully cut around the joint, working your way around the pelvis contours, keeping as much meat on the haunches as possible. NB: Check for scent glands near the anus (small light-brown or gray lumps) and ensure they are removed with the pelvis. They taste bad.

Finished Cuts

- **Rear haunches:** Meaty legs, ideal for roasting or braising. Can also be boned and diced.
- **Saddle:** Contains tender back meat, which can be boned and diced.
- **Front shoulders:** Not much meat on them but worth adding to a stew. Remove any remaining fur if not boning out.
- **Ribs:** Can be cooked in stock or stews.
- **Kidneys, liver, and heart:** Optional use.

Haunches (still need separating from pelvis), saddle, front legs, and ribs.

Preparing Other Mammals

A squirrel is prepared in a very similar way to a rabbit. You can roast them whole or joint for adding to a stew. Even larger mammals have a similar structure and can be dismantled in a similar way to the above method for a rabbit. Some have a lot more fat on them—for example, beaver—but are essentially the same structure. I wouldn't go to the trouble of jointing a mouse, though.

A deer has a very similar structure to a rabbit. It's just bigger and takes more work to dismantle.

Pot-roasted beaver joints.

Preparing Birds

Most of the meat on smaller birds such as pigeons or ptarmigans is on the breast. This is also the best meat. An easy way of harvesting this meat is to break the skin over the breastbone, pushing it down either side, then cut out the breast muscle. With larger birds, it's worth harvesting more of the meat from other parts of the body. In this case, start by plucking the feathers off.

1. **Plucking:** Start at the breast and work toward the tail and wings, gripping small sections of feathers and pulling firmly in the direction they grow. Continue until the bird is fully plucked. At first it seems like it will take forever, but soon you'll feel like you are making progress.
2. **Removing the head and feet:** Use a sharp knife or an axe to remove the head. Cut off the feet at the joint where the legs meet the scaly skin.
3. **Gutting:** Make a small incision at the base of the breastbone and extend it to the vent under the tail. Carefully reach inside to remove the internal organs. Take care not to puncture the intestines or stomach. Remove the crop from the neck area.
4. **Final cleaning:** Rinse the cavity thoroughly with water if you have some available. You can also rinse the outside to remove any remaining feathers or debris.

Plucking feathers from a pheasant.

In a fixed camp or cabin, you might have a large enough cast-iron pot to roast a bird whole. On self-propelled wilderness journeys, you likely won't. In the latter case, one option is to joint up the bird into breast, legs, and wings, then pan-fry or add to a casserole. With pheasants, it's worth stewing until the meat comes off the bone. An alternative method, especially useful if you don't have a pot, is to spatchcock the bird, placing it into a split stick and cooking it over a fire.

The fundamental idea with spatchcocking is to split the carcass up the middle, flatten it out, then grill it. If you are grilling the bird on a barbeque or on a grill over a fire, it doesn't matter if you split the bird up the backbone or up the breastbone. If you are cooking the bird in a split stick, it does matter. The stick holding the bird will mask any meat inside it. So, the spine should be in this space. Split the bird up the breast by taking a knife down the side of the sternum, leaving the breast meat intact. This allows the breast and the legs to be cooked well, which is necessary with fowl.

Spatchcocked birds roasting over coals.

Natural Navigation

Looking after yourself in the wilds, with minimal reliance on equipment but maximum reliance on your skills and knowledge of nature, includes being able to find your way.

In today's age of advanced technology, one might question the need for mastering traditional natural navigation techniques. However, these methods can, at the very least, serve as valuable checks and backups for modern devices as well as being able to bolster navigation with map and compass. These techniques are not mutually exclusive. You just need to know how to combine them harmoniously.

Natural navigation fosters self-reliance in its purest form. In addition to being a backup for modern devices when they break or run out of power, natural navigation skills have deeper ramifications for preserving our freedoms. Historically, most mapping was created by, or directly for, governments. Modern satellite navigation systems are vulnerable to spoofing and jamming. The natural phenomena on which natural navigation is based are out of reach of any political control, and the skills, once you have them, cannot be taken away.

There are many cues in nature from which we can gain information about direction. But the clearest, most consistent, and widely applicable natural indicators are the sun, moon, and stars.

THE THREE NORTHS

As navigators there are three norths we must juggle—geographic north, magnetic north, and grid north.

Geographic north: The geographic north pole, also known as true north, is the point where the earth's axis of rotation meets its surface in the Northern Hemisphere. The geographic north pole is the point in the north where lines of longitude converge. Similarly, lines of longitude also converge at the geographic south pole. A line of longitude passing through your position is known as your meridian. Following your meridian north would lead you to the geographic north pole. Following your meridian south would lead you to the geographic south pole. Therefore, your meridian is a north–south line through your position.

Magnetic north: The magnetic north pole is the point in the earth's Northern Hemisphere where its magnetic field points vertically downward. This pole is influenced by various factors that make up the earth's complex magnetic field. It is not in the same place as the geographic north pole. It should be noted that when you are using a compass, the compass needle does not point directly to the magnetic north pole. Rather, your compass needle aligns with the horizontal component of the earth's magnetic field at your position. The relationship between this local magnetic north indication and the other norths will be shown on the legend for the map you are using.

Grid north: This is a reference direction established on maps using a grid system. A rectilinear grid is overlaid on land maps and divided into progressively smaller grid squares to provide accurate location information, in the form of grid references. The US National Grid and the British National Grid are examples of such systems. Conventionally, grid north is at the top of a map. Mapping grid systems may be aligned to a line of longitude at their edge or their center, depending on how they are set to overlay an area of land. Other than where a north–south line of the grid coincides with a line of longitude, grid north will differ from true north. The relationship between grid north and true north is typically stated in a map's legend, or key. If lines of longitude are printed on the map, you can see the relationship between them and the map's grid directly on the map sheet.

Using the Three Norths

Natural navigation cues from primary indicators such as the sun and other celestial bodies, and secondary indicators such as the alignment of termite mounds (see page 200), all relate to geographic north and south. When you are using a map and compass, however, you are primarily concerned with grid north, magnetic north, and the relationship between them. If you are using your compass along with natural cues, you are concerned with the relationship between magnetic north and geographic north. If you are using your map along with natural cues, you are concerned with the relationship between grid north and geographic north.

Knowing the relationship between the three norths is essential for accurate navigation using maps and compasses. This information allows you to walk in straight lines and find your way, even when your destination is not visible. Local topographic maps usually provide information on the relationship between magnetic north and grid north for the area covered, but it is essential to ensure this information is up to date, since magnetic declination varies over time.

You can use natural navigation cues in conjunction with your map-and-compass navigation. You will have more tools in your navigational toolbox, and you'll have more information to help you remain oriented and on course. To do so, you need to know the relationship between geographic north and the other two norths for the locality in which you are operating. This information can usually be found in the key of your map.

If you don't have a map, you don't need to worry about grid north, since it exists only on the map. If you have a compass, though, you need to remember that your compass aligns with the local magnetic field; it does not point to geographic north. If there is significant magnetic declination in the area in which you are operating, there will be a significant difference between the direction your compass needle is pointing and the direction of geographic north, which you will achieve through natural navigation techniques.

Natural navigation techniques, such as using the sun, moon, and stars to determine direction, can also help in understanding the relationship between the different norths. For example, finding Polaris, the North Star, will help find geographic north. With this knowledge and a compass, the difference between geographic north and magnetic north can be determined for your position. Thus, you could measure the local magnetic declination for your area. This would then allow for more-accurate navigation, using your compass alongside natural navigation techniques. You can also use your compass to check the accuracy of your natural navigation when you are learning or training. You just need to know the relationship between magnetic north and geographic north in the locality, so you can translate between the two.

Understanding the three norths—geographic, magnetic, and grid north—is fundamental to accurate and effective navigation. By familiarizing yourself with these modalities of north and their relationships, you can enhance your navigation skills and become more adept at finding your way, regardless of the tools or techniques you choose to use.

Map and compass navigation relates grid north to magnetic north, while natural navigation indicators relate to true north.

FINDING DIRECTION FROM THE SUN

The (apparent) motion of the sun is by far and away the most useful to understand for the purposes of natural navigation. It's very regular, therefore predictable. Understanding this provides a globally relevant foundation to orient oneself. It will also help interpret secondary localized direction indicators, many of which are influenced by exposure to sunlight. A natural navigator needs to understand the daily and annual motion of the sun. The first relates to the fact that the earth is rotating on its axis; the second relates to the fact that the earth orbits the sun.

We use the phrase *apparent motion* because the motion we observe is due to the motion of the earth, not the sun. The daily motion of the sun through our skies is due to the earth's rotation. The changes in position of the sun over the course of a year, along with the seasons, are due to the earth orbiting the sun, combined with the earth's axis of rotation being tilted compared to the plane of its orbit around the sun.

Northern Hemisphere fall and winter occur while geographic north is tilted away from the sun. At the same time, geographic south is tilted toward the sun and brings the Southern Hemisphere spring and summer. Conversely, Northern Hemisphere spring and summer occur while geographic north is tilted toward the sun, with geographic south being tilted away and Southern Hemisphere fall and winter occurring.

At the equinoxes, in March and September, neither geographic north nor geographic south is tilted toward or away from the sun. That is, the earth's axis of rotation is tilted neither toward nor away from the sun. In simple and practical terms, this means on the days of the equinoxes, the sun rises east and sets west. Also, on these days, at noon on the equator, the sun is directly overhead. On any other days of the year these statements are not true, or at least not accurate.

Most of us have known the adage that the sun rises in the east and sets in the west for so long that we can't remember where we first heard it. In fact, this is where the linkage between the east—or the Orient—and "to orient oneself" derives. Somewhat like a stopped clock being correct twice a day, however, this adage is correct only twice a year, on the days of the equinoxes. During the rest of the year, the sun sets and rises north or south of these points, due to the axial tilt of the earth. This is linked to the length of the day at a given latitude, with the sun spending more time above the horizon as the days get longer.

Looking east at sunrise? Broadly yes, but here the view is significantly north of east, along the southwestern coast of Portugal in July.

Lest the previous make you feel less confident about gaining direction from the sun, there's also a limit to how far away from east your sunrise can be and how far away from west your sunset can be. The sun will always rise somewhere in the eastern part of the sky and always set somewhere in the western part of the sky. Moreover, it's very predictable where that will be—it doesn't change very much from one day to the next. Even if you are far enough away from the equator that on some summer days the sun never sets (inside the Arctic or Antarctic Circle), the sun will still be rising away from the horizon in the eastern part of the sky, reaching maximum height at local noon, then dropping toward the horizon again in the western part of the sky.

Using a Sun Stick

So, let's now think about what the sun does during the day and how we might make use of this. As the sun tracks west, shadows track east. We can use this to our advantage with the simple and classic sun stick. Simply place a stick in the ground, mark the end of the shadow, and wait a while for the shadow to move a noticeable amount—maybe thirty minutes. Mark the end of the shadow a second time. Since the shadow will have tracked from west to east, the line between your markers will be an *approximate* east–west line.

Two markers, placed thirty minutes apart, give an approximate east–west line.

A third marker was placed three hours fifteen minutes after a first, giving a more accurate east–west line.

With a longer wait, the line becomes a better approximation, and this technique can provide a very accurate result. It is also more accurate if you take two measurements on either side of local noon, rather than both before, or both after, local noon. Once you have your east–west line, you can draw a line at right angles to give a north–south line.

Understanding Local Noon

These days we tend to think of noon as 12:00 on our watches. The definition of local noon, also known as solar noon, is defined as the time at which the sun crosses your meridian. So, local noon is specific to your longitude—how far east or west you are. Picture a globe with lines of longitude running from geographic north to geographic south. These are meridians. From your perspective, at the point the sun crosses your meridian it is at the highest point above your horizon for that day. Before local noon the sun is rising, and after local noon it is falling. Local noon is also when your shadow will be shortest.

Since local noon is defined as the time at which the sun crosses your meridian, the imaginary north–south line that runs under your feet, your shadow at noon will coincide with this north–south line. Equally, at local noon, a linear shadow, such as that of a straight stick, also falls on a north–south line. More directly, at local noon, the position of the sun provides an accurate indicator of south or north.

At local noon, as the sun crosses your meridian, it will be on an imaginary north–south line running through your position.

In areas north of the Tropic of Cancer—which includes most of Eurasia and all of North America apart from the southern portion of Mexico—the sun will always be south of directly overhead, even at local noon (at which time it will indicate south). South of the Tropic of Capricorn, the sun will always be north of directly overhead, even at local noon (at which time it will indicate north).

Thinking back to our sun stick method, it's possible you have noticed a potential problem with it. The length of the shadow will be changing as the height of the sun above the horizon varies. Only if you placed your first marker a given amount of time *before* local noon and your second marker the same length of time *after* local noon would you get an exact east–west line over a relatively short period of time. But we can use the symmetry that exists around local noon to our advantage. If you know the time of local noon, simply place your first marker, say, twenty minutes before, and your second marker twenty minutes after. If you want to work out the time of local noon, you must observe the time when the shadow of your stick is shortest (the day before).

If you don't have a watch, or you haven't yet worked out the clock time of local noon (it's unlikely to be 12:00), then this symmetry around local noon can be used in a different way with your sun stick. In the morning, draw a circle around your sun stick (a piece of string fixed to the stick can be used to measure the radius). Size the circle so that the end of the shadow is falling a little way outside the circle. As the sun rises higher in the sky, the shadow will shorten as well as moving east to west. Mark where the end of the shadow crosses the circle. Later, mark where the end of the shadow crosses back outside the circle again as the shadow lengthens. The line between the two points will be an exact east–west line. If you do have a watch and you record the times the shadow crosses the circle, you'll also be able to work out the time of local noon—it will be the time exactly halfway between the two times you recorded.

Another Problem with Time

The general sun stick method is reasonably accurate. The circle and shadow-stick method is more accurate. But the problem with either is that they require you to stay in one place for quite a while. It's possible you need to be on the move; you are navigating, after all. So, we need some other ways of using the sun too.

The earth rotates once per day. This is the definition of a day. So, due to the rotation of the earth, the sun apparently moves through 360 degrees over a twenty-four-hour period. That is an average of 15 degrees per hour.

Once you know the time of local noon, you can work out direction from the sun at any time of the day if you have a watch. For example, you are north of the Tropics and local noon is 12:09. The time is currently 10:15, so the sun will be approximately 30 degrees east of south. Stated another way, you know where the sun is, and so south will be 30 degrees ahead of the sun's current position. Just less than two hours later, the sun will be directly south. After another three hours of walking, the sun will be 45 degrees past south; that is, it will be indicating southwest. You don't need to stop very long to use this method to work out the cardinal directions. You can combine this with other indicators too, particularly as you walk to maintain course.

FINDING DIRECTION FROM THE STARS

There is a rich history of humans navigating by the stars. Much of this was based on extensive observation and record keeping of one form or another, whether by oral traditions of native peoples or the meticulous records of the seventeenth-century astronomer John Flamsteed.

Before this puts you off, let me offer a simple observation—the sun is a star. Admittedly, it is a star with which we have a special relationship. But the reason the sun rises, moves across the sky, and sets again is because the earth is rotating, not because we are on one of the sun's satellites.

So it is with other stars—if they appear to be rising, then we are looking eastward; if they appear to be setting, then we are looking westward. They also track across the sky in a similar manner to the sun. So, if we are in the Northern Hemisphere and we see stars moving from left to right, then we are facing southward. If we are in the Southern Hemisphere and we see stars moving from right to left, then we are looking northward.

If we can recognize specific stars or groupings of stars, then we can be more accurate in their use. For example, Mintaka, one of the stars in the belt of Orion, lies on the celestial equator. This means it always rises at the east point on the horizon and sets at the west point.

Polaris, the North Star

Polaris, also known as the Pole Star or the North Star, is a crucial celestial marker for navigation. This is because Polaris is pretty much on the earth's axis of rotation, meaning that this star marks the north celestial pole. Polaris appears stationary in the night sky, since everything else rotates around it. In other words, it sits directly above Earth's geographic north pole. This means that you can use Polaris to determine geographic north. Once you have found Polaris, extend an imaginary line from the star down to the horizon, meeting it at right angles. This gives true north.

To find Polaris, one typically uses an asterism, which forms part of the constellation Ursa Major, known as the Plough or the Big Dipper Two of the stars—Dubhe and Merak—known as the pointers, point toward Polaris. By extending an imaginary line beyond these stars, approximately five times the distance between them, you will find Polaris.

The highly recognizable constellation Orion rising from the east. Manitoba, Canada.

Long-exposure photo showing rotation of stars around the north celestial pole.

Cassiopeia is another helpful constellation for finding Polaris. It's a recognizable constellation that sits within the Milky Way, with a W or M shape, depending on its orientation. The open side of Cassiopeia's W always faces toward Polaris. If you draw a line across the open side of the W, then extend a second line at right angles, for approximately twice the distance as measured across the mouth, you'll find Polaris.

Another, sometimes useful, observation regarding Polaris is that the height of Polaris above the horizon in degrees is equal to your latitude. At the equator, Polaris is on the horizon, and with increasing northerly latitudes, it is correspondingly higher in the sky, until you arrive at the geographic north pole with Polaris directly overhead, or 90 degrees above the horizon.

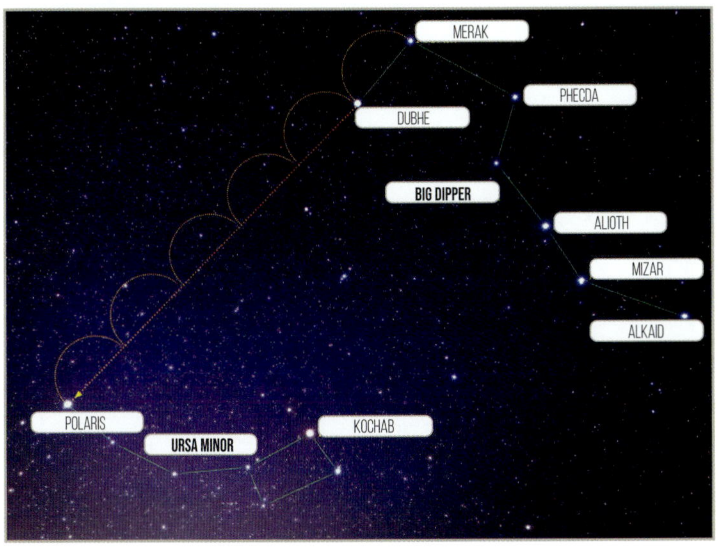

Finding Polaris from the Big Dipper.

Crux, the Southern Cross

In the Southern Hemisphere, there is no analogous star to Polaris, marking the celestial pole. But we can use the Southern Cross, the constellation Crux, to help find the south celestial pole. Once you have found the south celestial pole, like finding north in the Northern Hemisphere, draw an imaginary line straight down from the celestial pole to the horizon, meeting the horizon at right angles. This spot on the horizon is your direction for true south.

To find south using the Southern Cross, start by making sure you have the Southern Cross, not one of the false crosses. To do this, use the pointers, two bright stars (Alpha and Beta Centauri) near the Southern Cross. Their presence will confirm you have the correct cross-shaped constellation, Crux. Crux consists of four main stars forming a cross shape with a long axis and a short axis. The long axis will help you determine south.

Using only Crux: Extend an imaginary line through the two stars of the long axis, continuing this line about four and a half times the length of the cross itself. At the end of this extension, you'll reach a point in the sky in the vicinity of the south celestial pole.

Using the pointers: In addition to the imaginary line from Crux, you can create an imaginary line from the points, which will help determine the area of the south celestial pole. First draw an imaginary line between the pointers. Second, starting in the middle of the first imaginary line, draw a second imaginary line at right angles to the first, extending it until it intersects with the imaginary line from Crux described above. Where the two lines intersect is the area of the south celestial pole. Now draw your line down the horizon to gain the south point.

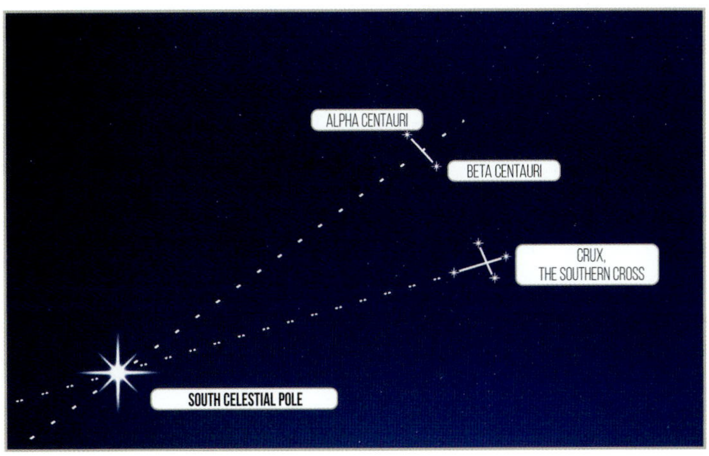

Using Crux and the pointers in combination.

FINDING DIRECTION FROM THE MOON

The motion of the moon is relatively complex compared to other celestial bodies, but we can still make use of it for navigation. We need one simple observation: The illuminated part of the moon is reflecting light emanating from the sun. We understand the motion of the sun, particularly daily. Telling direction from the moon flows from being able to tell direction from the sun. Even if the sun is below the horizon, the moon will indicate the position of the sun.

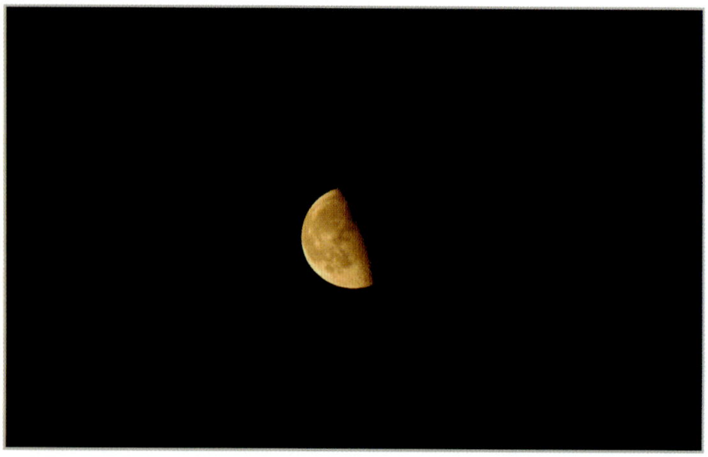

The observation that the light reflected by the illuminated part of the moon comes from the sun is of great use to the natural navigator.

The easiest example to understand first is that of a full moon. For the disc of the moon to be fully illuminated, it must be opposite the sun; that is, 180 degrees between them. If you are facing a full moon, the sun is behind you. A full moon will rise as the sun is setting. We can go further too, on the basis of the knowledge of the sun's motion in this chapter. Just as the sun is directly over your meridian at local noon, so will a full moon be over your meridian at local midnight, which is twelve hours after (or before) local noon.

A new or waxing crescent moon is always going to appear to be in the sky not far behind the sun, traveling east to west. The illuminated sliver of moon will of course be facing the sun. Similarly, an old or waning crescent moon will be visible not long before sunrise, appearing just ahead of the sun. If you draw an imaginary line across the horns of a crescent moon and extend the line to the horizon, it will give you an indication of south in the Northern Hemisphere, and north in the Southern Hemisphere.

The illuminated part of this waxing crescent moon in the early evening gives away the position of the sun, which is below the horizon to the west; a line across the horns of the moon extended downward toward the horizon indicates south. Ontario, Canada.

A waning crescent moon in the predawn sky. The sun is below the horizon to the east, and a line across the horns of the moon extended down to the horizon indicates south. Manitoba, Canada.

Full moon rising 180 degrees from where the sun set. This was less than two weeks before the September equinox. The sun would have set slightly north of west, so the moon rose slightly south of east. Manitoba, Canada.

ADDITIONAL DIRECTION INDICATORS

The Shape of Trees

Trees are shaped by their environment, and several aspects of this can be useful for establishing cardinal directions. Trees gain energy from the sun. Broad-leaved deciduous trees will tend to put more foliage on the sunward side. In the Northern Hemisphere this will be to the south, while in the Southern Hemisphere this will be to the north. Branches on the sunward side will tend to have a greater horizontal component than branches on the opposite side of the tree, which tend to have a greater vertical component. Sunward branches can also be longer. So, if you are looking at the tree from east or west, the tree branches will tend to create a checkmark shape. This is most clearly seen in mature trees that are not in the shadow of other trees.

Checkmark tree in the Northern Hemisphere. The more horizontal branches and greater amount of foliage are to the south. The more upright branches are to the north.

Wind can complicate the shape of a tree, making it harder to see the effects of the sun. A strong and consistent prevailing wind will shape a tree such that the direction of the wind is obvious, even on a calm day. With knowledge of the prevailing wind direction, trees will exhibit this direction to you. From this it is simple to work out cardinal directions.

Looking south toward exposed trees that are noticeably shaped by a prevailing westerly wind.

Wood Ants: Boreal Forests

It's generally true that if an anthill is located near a large tree in the northern forests, the nest will be somewhere on the sunny side of the tree, which will be the southern side. They can often be shifted toward the southeast, benefiting from morning sun after a cold night. But local shade from other trees is a significant factor in the exact positioning of a nest. Also, you can encounter nests in clearings, not particularly close to any one tree, which is less indicative of direction. In my experience, it's best to cross-check any direction indication from anthills with other indicators.

Wood ant nest in northern Sweden.

Termite Mounds: Australia

Termite mounds in northern Australia can be used to ascertain cardinal directions. The longer, thinner edge of the mound aligns north–south and the broad sides face east–west; this orientation helps regulate the temperature within the mound by minimizing sun exposure during the hottest part of the day (around noon) but gaining more sun exposure in the cooler parts of the day (morning and evening).

Termite mounds in evening light. Queensland, Australia.

Termite Mounds: Southern Africa

In southern Africa, mounds of termites in the genus *Macrotermes* are useful for establishing direction. These termites consume plant material indirectly through the cultivation of fungus within the mound. Unlike some other types of termite mound, they don't have visible ventilation holes at the top. Rather, they are built to a sort of pinnacle. The useful observation is the pinnacle leans in the direction of north to north-northwest. The simplest explanation is that the material on the side that gains more sun dries more quickly and more completely than the side that is shaded. There are also some other theories, however, including one regarding the average zenith angle of the sun. The important point, however, is that in southern Africa these termite mounds indicate north.

The shape of the tree corroborates north with the termite mound. South Africa.

The lopsided pinnacle of this termite mound indicates north.

Other Effects of the Sun

Termite mounds prove to be very reliable indicators of direction. Other natural navigation indicators also relate to the effect of the sun; for example, moss growing on cooler, shaded sides of trees, or where frost persists in shadow on a sunny winter's day. Understand the motion of the sun, and your understanding of many other indicators will also snap into place. But do bear in mind that local factors, particularly shade and local microclimates, can have a significant bearing on what presents itself to you.

Moss growing on only the north side of a tree. East Sussex, UK.

Aurora

The aurora borealis, commonly known as the northern lights, is a natural phenomenon observed at high latitudes. They are caused by solar wind interacting with Earth's magnetic field and atmosphere. Indigenous peoples such as the Sami and Inuit have long used auroras for navigation. Auroras can be either diffuse or distinct, with the latter typically appearing as east–west-aligned curtains or bands. This east–west alignment is useful for orientation.

Use Everything You Can

As you can see in the above photos of termite mounds or aurora, there are several natural direction indicators corroborating. Whenever you are navigating and whichever means you are using, you should always use multiple indicators if possible. This helps highlight localized idiosyncrasies affecting one of the indicators. If indicators appear to contradict each other, then this is the time to check everything. If you rely on only one directional cue, then you are more likely to be misled or make a mistake. Moreover, when you are learning, it's always good to double-check to make sure you have understood properly, made your observations or calculations accurately, and applied the technique correctly.

Aurora to the north, spanning the sky east–west. The Big Dipper is indicating Polaris (top center). Ontario, Canada.

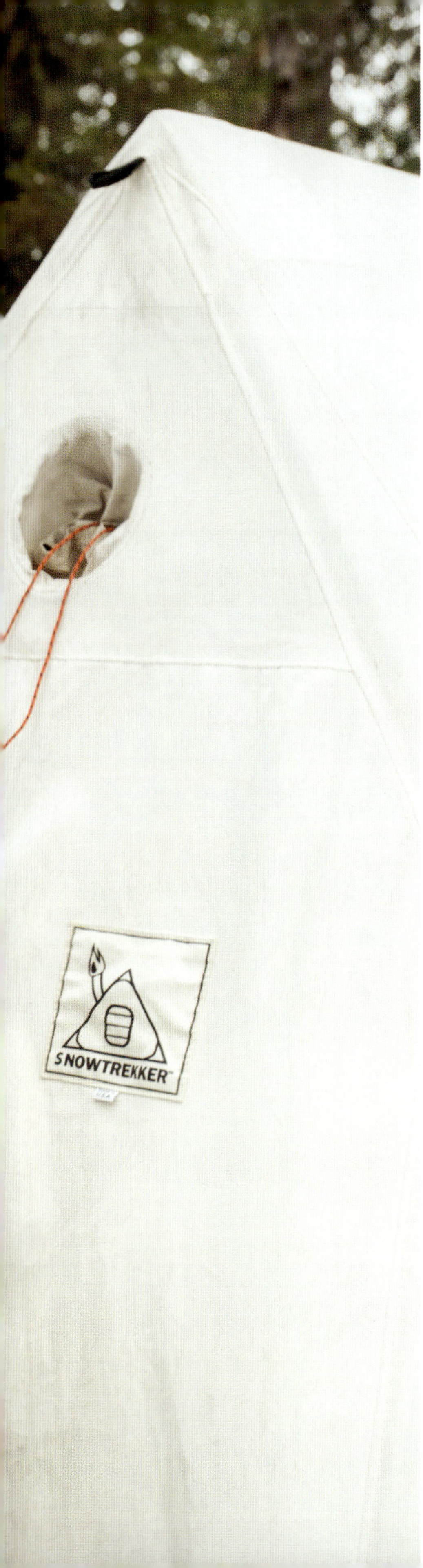

Clothing and Equipment

At the heart of bushcraft is a practical knowledge of nature. While the focus of bushcraft is not equipment, some supplies make the application of your knowledge and skills a lot easier and other aspects of your trips quicker or more comfortable. Even so, you should avoid the "everything but the kitchen sink" approach. Except for emergency items, such as first-aid kits, the discipline of packing well for a trip relies on leaving things out, rather than including items just in case.

You can build redundancy into your kit by choosing items that will not rapidly degrade, are field maintainable, and are unlikely to break under the demands of your trip. Of course, these considerations should be balanced with ensuring the total weight of your gear is not excessive.

KEY PIECES OF PERSONAL EQUIPMENT

In the context of exercising bushcraft skills, some items of equipment naturally come to the top of the kit list for any forest or bush environment. This is whether you are out for a day or a month.

Core items for forest and bush. Note the ferro rod striker has a whistle in it.

A fixed-blade knife, a folding saw, and a ferro rod are vital. If you are taking a knife, you should carry a small sharpening stone. Hydration is always a necessity, so a water container is needed too. A metal mug allows you to boil water. A mug that nests inside your bottle is ideal. Include a headlamp, which allows you to operate beyond daylight. Carrying additional, varied fire-lighting means is also prudent, such as a butane lighter and a waterproof match case. While you can make cordage, it takes time. It's always handy to have a length of strong cord with you for immediate use. Remember, cord acts as backup fire-making equipment too.

Bottle nested with metal mug.

Whatever the size of belt knife you carry, a pocketknife is useful and can also act as a backup to your main cutting tool. When you carry a knife, you should carry a cuts kit in your pocket. It can also be handy for other small cuts, burns, thorns, etc. If you are working with a larger cutting tool such as an axe or parang, it's sensible to bring a trauma bandage and a tourniquet.

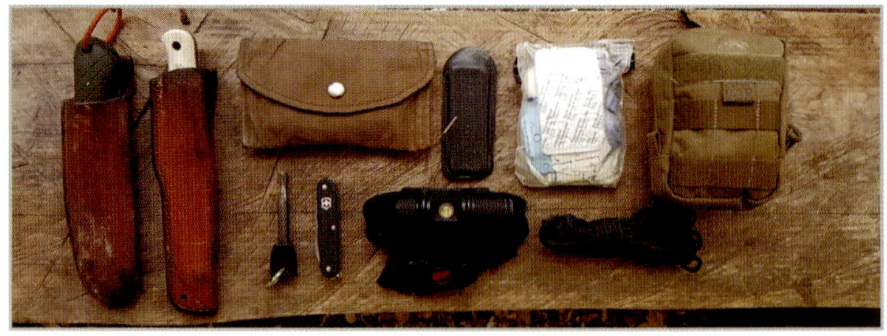

Clockwise from left: folding saw, belt knife, tinder pouch, sharpening stone, cuts kit, pouch containing trauma dressing and tourniquet, paracord, headlamp, pocketknife, ferro rod.

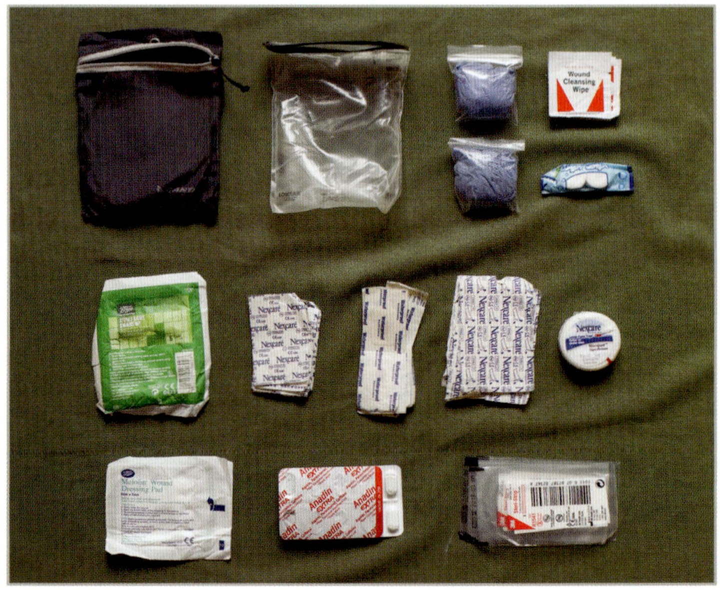

Pocket first-aid kit contents for cuts and other minor injuries, containing an assortment of small wound coverings and closures, wipes, gauze, tape, nitrile gloves, analgesics, and a waterproof pouch.

In my experience, there are a few pieces of clothing and equipment that will make or break time spent outdoors—waterproof shell layers, footwear, and sleeping equipment. Many of the places we might venture into the wilds in the temperate world, as well as subtropical and boreal environments, demand that we protect ourselves, and our warm layers of clothing, from wet precipitation. These places are potentially cool enough that getting wet will be a problem. To avoid hypothermia in these places, proper rain gear is essential.

We can reasonably say that when outdoors, we will either be in our boots or in our beds. If either are inadequate, they can make a trip miserable. Hence, you should pay close attention to ensuring your footwear and sleeping equipment are specified correctly for your intended trip. This includes keeping this equipment in good condition in the field. I would also caution against overspecification, which I have seen novices do in the realm of sleeping gear—taking kit that is too warm and many pounds over the weight they could be carrying. I'm often asked what the best sleeping bag is. Unfortunately, if you intend to visit wild places across different seasons, latitudes, or both, you will have to invest in a range of different sleeping setups.

Left: Invest in high-quality footwear and keep it in good condition. Right: Lightweight sleeping kit—sleeping mat, sleeping bag, bivvy bag, and tarp—just right for summer.

If you are journeying, then navigation equipment should also be high on your list of items that make a considerable difference to your ability to operate and stay safe in a wild environment. A local map is the most essential item, then a compass. A watch is handy for timing navigation legs. While not essential, binoculars can help with route finding, as well as wildlife watching.

Reliable personal equipment items used on many wilderness trips.

Implicit in all the above is that these pieces of equipment should be easily carried with you. Your equipment shouldn't hinder you. The essential equipment you choose should be light and comfortable enough that you are never tempted to leave it behind at times when you should have it with you. Further, all the above items of equipment should be of as high a quality as you can afford.

A MODULAR SYSTEM FOR KIT

By definition, your key pieces of kit shouldn't change much whether you are going out for an afternoon or a week. Some trips, you may swap out one knife for another, for example, but you'll still take a knife. Clearly, if you are out for the day, you don't need sleeping kit, but the rest of your key items are useful whenever you are out. In this sense, I consider these items the core module. For longer periods out, I will add other modules. In this sense we can consider sleeping kit as another module. Of course, we may also have multiple modules that serve the same purpose but under different conditions. Staying with the example of sleeping kit, for summer adventures we might have a light bivvy bag, short sleeping mat, two-season down sleeping bag, and small, light silicone nylon tarp. For cooler, potentially wetter, conditions such as late fall or early spring in a temperate climate, we might take a larger tarp, three-four-season sleeping bag, larger bivvy bag to accommodate the sleeping bag, and a full-length sleeping pad. A modular system allows everything to dovetail nicely. Combining items of equipment into functional modules (another would be cooking equipment) allows you to pack and organize your gear faster at home, as well as in the field.

CLOTHING PRINCIPLES

Very specific environmental advice on clothing is beyond the scope of what I have room for in this book, but I will share with you some general principles that will be useful.

First, recognize that **however technical, or expensive, a garment, much of the performance you can gain from it will be down to your management of your clothing and yourself**. No waterproof jacket will put itself on you when it starts to rain. Any hood on a jacket or fleece must be manually operated by you. Gloves and hats don't put themselves on and off.

Avoid overheating. This applies in cold climates as well as hot ones. Fundamentally, you may have to regulate your activity, especially in warm climates. In cooler climates, wearing too many clothes can mean you overheat when exerting yourself. Better to start walking up a hill, or chopping wood, feeling a little chilly then come up to temperature, than starting warm then overheating: **Be bold, start cold**. The issue with overheating is sweat. If you sweat into clothes in cold conditions, you reduce the effectiveness of your insulative clothing and will become cold when you stop working as hard.

Ventilate. To shed excess heat quickly, actively ventilate—raise up your warm hat or take it off, open your collar, open front zips, use armpit zips, use zips down the side of pants, roll up sleeves, hold your shirt or base layer with both hands at the front, and waft air out under your collar or around your waist.

Organize clothing in layers. Having multiple garments of different levels of insulation (including hats and gloves/mittens) allows fine-tuning of your insulation. You can increase insulation in colder conditions, or you can reduce insulation if it is warmer or you are working hard. Multiple layers of clothing allow you to select the best materials for each job; for example, in extremely cold, dry conditions, wool underwear and pullovers for insulating layers and a windproof cotton outer shell. For wet-cold conditions, fewer insulating layers and a Gore-Tex or similar breathable waterproof shell would be more appropriate.

Base layers. In cool conditions, wear an insulative base layer of merino wool, not cotton. Cotton is cold when it is damp. In hot environments, though, there is benefit to wearing cotton next to your skin. Long sleeves are often best, even in hot conditions, for sun protection. Also, consider thicker cotton for protection from biting insects such as mosquitoes or tsetse flies, or thorns in the bush.

Keep dry or keep dry clothes. In cool environments, you should do your utmost to keep your clothing dry, from either perspiration or environmental moisture. In hot, humid climates, you may have no choice but for your daytime clothing to become wet due to the ambient conditions, your exertions, or both. In the latter circumstance, you should keep dry clothing for the evenings and put on your wet clothing again the next day. If there is danger of you falling into water when being wet, and cold will be an issue—for example, on a canoe trip outside the height of summer, then carry a dry bag of dry, warm clothing.

Loose clothing is often best. In cold conditions, tight clothing can hinder blood circulation, as well as hinder warm air moving around your layers. In hot conditions, loose clothing will help airflow keep you cool.

Look after your clothing. Try to keep it as clean as possible and repair it when damaged. Dirt and grease degrade the performance of garments. On trips, include a small sewing kit in your repair kit.

ON-PERSON KIT

There are situations while traveling in wild places when you might not have access to your main bags or backpack; for example, when in helicopters or light planes. On a vehicle-based trip, maybe on a safari, for example, you might take an extended walk from the vehicle with your guide. Even going for a short walk away from a camp in remote country, to collect firewood, for example, you should consider the consequences of getting lost in unfamiliar territory. Further, there are numerous emergency situations you can envisage where you could lose your main equipment, such as slipping over and losing your backpack while wading across a river, or in capsizing a canoe. Then what you have on your person is critical.

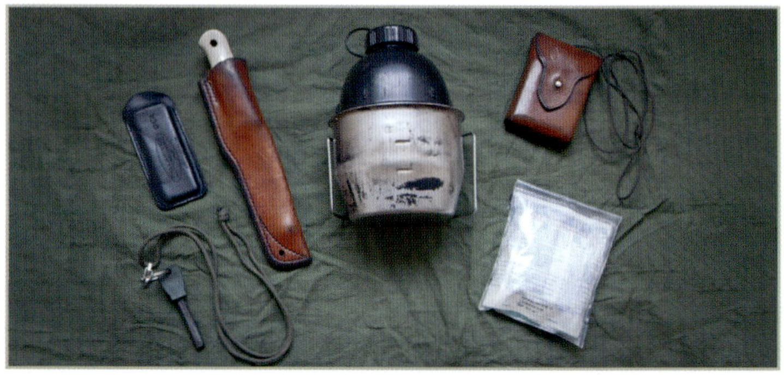

These are items you might want to carry when walking away from a bush camp or safari vehicle, even without a day pack.

Of course, you can't keep all your gear on your person all the time. It's simply not practical. It might even be unsafe to have too much equipment attached to your person; for example, in the case of a canoe capsize. Hence you need to make a considered decision about what to have on your person on different types of trips. This principle marries with the concept of layering gear. The inner layer is on your person. The next layer might be in a day pack.

In the context of being lost or stranded, as well as having key pieces of equipment for you to help yourself in the bush, as discussed above, having means of signaling or simply attracting attention to yourself will be invaluable. A whistle, a mirror, and a bright LED flashlight all are worth having on your person. While some gear such as ferro rod strikers have emergency whistles in them, a whistle such as used by a sports referee is louder. Sighting compasses have a mirror inside the lid and can be used to reflect sunlight. Lightweight emergency signaling mirrors are also available.

DAY PACK

The primary items you will pack for a day hike are the things you'll need for your hike in the environment you are walking through, including any likely weather changes. But it is worth being aware of the day hiker's paradox. When you head out for the day, the implicit assumption is that you will be back to your base camp, vehicle, or home by nightfall. If you head out for a multiday backpacking trip, with all the camping gear you need, if you don't get as far as you intend, you just set up camp anyway and try to make up for it in the coming days. If you head out for only the day and don't get as far as you intend, you have a bigger problem. Further, there are many more who will go for a day hike than are willing, or confident enough, to undertake an overnight backpacking trip.

Hence, the day hiker who finds themselves stuck out overnight is likely to be not only light on useful equipment, but also more likely to be relatively inexperienced. Moreover, even most avid campers have never spent the night out without camping equipment. Most news stories about lost hikers seem to be in relation to people who intended to be out only for the day, or even part of the day. The paradox, then, is that the people who are most likely to end up stuck out overnight are those who are least equipped to deal with it.

Packing for a day hike is a fine balance between keeping weight down and being prepared for a range of eventualities.

Clearly, for a day hike you are not going to pack a large rucksack full of everything you might need on a multiday trip. One of the joys of taking a day hike is being relatively light and nimble on your feet. But it's certainly worth packing items that would help you get out of any likely scrapes you might find yourself in. Carrying a few additional items in case of delays, poor weather, and the onset of nightfall can make all the difference. Carrying a bright LED headlamp and spare batteries alone can make the difference between arriving home late and spending the night out in the open. In addition to your core personal items of equipment, there are a few basic things worth packing in case you are delayed, encounter bad weather, or must spend the night out:

- **Food for the day plus a little bit extra**, such as a few additional snack bars or chocolate bars.
- **Water** (and a means of making some more). Take some means of collecting and purifying water appropriate to your environment. For example, this might be chlorine dioxide, which weighs very little but can sterilize more than 100 pints (60 liters) of water, or it could be a transpiration bag.
- **Shell layer**. Even if the weather is forecast to be good, in many environments it's prudent to take a waterproof jacket, which will also help keep you warm by trapping air inside your layers. Further, cool overnight temperatures sometimes bring on rain.
- **Warm layers**. Take a warm layer for during the day if needed but also an extra lightweight fleece in case you end up out after dark, when the temperature is likely to be lower than daytime. Add to this a warm hat and a head-over or buff for significant extra warmth for little extra weight.
- **Emergency shelter**. This is the one that many people neglect to take. Carry something appropriate to the environment. In the woods, a lightweight silicone nylon tarp will be useful even for rainy lunch stops but can also form the basis of an overnight shelter. As discussed in the shelter chapter, survival bags are versatile, and brightly colored bags or tarps are useful for attracting attention.
- **Headlamp**. After dark this will be invaluable for finding your way, reading a map, or attracting attention. Carry spare batteries too.

BACKPACK

If you intend to spend some nights camping, you'll likely be packing some sleeping kit and a few more items of gear as well as some food, in addition to what you might have in your day pack. This is likely, then, to need a pack bigger than your day pack. In essence, though, via the principles of layering and taking a modular approach, what is below is largely built on the above. The following kit is an example of what works well as a three-season temperate outfit. Don't see this as something you must rigidly replicate, though; there are many valid variations of this.

1. Sleeping bag. Three-season.
2. Sleeping mat. Three-quarter length to save weight and space.
3. Bivvy bag
4. Tarp. Large for plenty of room. Will sleep two people.
5. Rucksack
6. Waterproof (submersible) rucksack liner
7. Billy can
8. Water filter
9. Spoon
10. Water bottle and metal mug
11. Second water bottle
12. Bathroom kit, containing toilet paper, wet wipes, alcohol hand gel, and butane lighter for burning toilet paper
13. Wash kit
14. Waterproof jacket and pants
15. Heavier warm layer
16. Spare clothes—socks, underwear, and T-shirt
17. Lightweight warm layer in stuff sack, which also can hold 18, 19, and 20
18. Bandana. This has lots of uses, from a scarf to a towel to a rough water filter to an emergency triangular bandage.
19. Wool hat
20. Sun hat
21. Head torch (flashlight)
22. Axe
23. Belt knife
24. Folding saw
25. Ferro rod
26. "Possibles pouch." This can contain essential items such as matches, butane lighter, sharpening stone if not in pockets, but also a repair kit, fishing kit, insect repellent, and other small items useful or essential to your trip. Such a kit can be slipped on your belt when you are away from camp.
27. First-aid kit. More substantial than a pocket kit.
28. Map and map case
29. Compass
30. Notebook and cover
31. Binoculars

All the above kit plus some food packed into the rucksack.

A versatile three-season woodland camping outfit.

Paul Kirtley is one of the world's leading bushcraft educators and authors. Through his school, Frontier Bushcraft, he offers bushcraft and survival courses, wilderness expeditions, and online training resources. Kirtley has taught wilderness skills around the world since 2003.

He produces the Paul Kirtley wilderness skills podcast and contributes to a range of magazines, books, and online resources focused on bushcraft, survival, and scouting skills. He is also the author of *Wilderness Axe Skills and Campcraft*.

www.paulkirtley.co.uk